THE INCLUSION SOLUTION

My Big Six Formula for Success

D.A. ABRAMS

Ingram Edition 2019
Second Edition, *The Inclusion Solution*
First Edition, as *Diversity & Inclusion: The Bix Six Formula for Success*, 2013
ISBN: 978-1-4910-1008-2

TABLE OF CONTENTS

INTRODUCTION TO THE NEW EDITION

DIVERSITY AND INCLUSION have been in the news a great deal this year, from the #OscarsSoWhite campaign to the issues around Ferguson, Freddie Gray, Black Lives Matter, and Blue Lives Matters, from a heightened awareness of politicians' positions on issues of diversity to rapidly developing policies on state and local inclusion efforts for transgender school children and adults.

This heightened awareness of the complex issues around diversity and inclusion along with an expanded public awareness of discrepancies, regulations, and potential for economic and social success led me to revisit this book and update it.

This new edition still has at its core my Big Six Formula for implementing concrete change in the diversity and inclusion policies and procedures of any corporation, organization, or non-profit NGO. It still goes into depth on the approach, its rationale, and the steps for applying it to any executive's staff and executive structure. It also offers a wealth of current data, many new case studies, and a deeper analysis of the application of my Inclusion Solution for broadest bottom-line impact.

In the few years since my first edition of this book, while I have seen solid developments and great role models, I also continue to see companies, organizations, and executives who find "winning at diversity" to be a challenge for them and their institutions. As *The Huffington Post* noted in May 2016, "the inclusion puzzle has confounded countless companies striving to cultivate a culture that values people from all backgrounds and abilities."[1] That makes the need for *The Inclusion Solution* still great. What this new edition can share, however, is an expanded focus on those companies that are already working towards cultivating a more diverse workforce and the benefits they are reaping. These include "improved morale, broader perspectives, more authentic marketing and brand positions, and ... a healthier bottom line."

I know you will find this book to be a great resource, whether you're approaching D&I fresh within your organization or if you have been responsible for addressing these issues in the past. Whether this is your first time reading it or if you are revisiting it for the updates and enhancements, I am sure you will find something stimulating and actionable in this new edition of *The Inclusion Solution*.

INTRODUCTION

WHEN A LATINO media executive was driving down Sunset Boulevard in Hollywood, California, he noticed an enormous new billboard for a Fortune 500 company that advertised children's clothing. The artwork featured two adorable white babies, dressed in white outfits lolling on a white blanket with white letters above them shaped like white clouds. It was a beautiful billboard. But it struck him as odd, given the demographics of the community over which it towered.

The executive immediately put in a call to Dr. David Hayes-Bautista, Director of the Center for the Study of Latino Health and Culture at UCLA's School of Medicine and renowned expert on Los Angeles's population. Dr. Hayes-Bautista confirmed what the executive suspected: the percentage of babies born in L.A. in 2012—the billboard's target "customer"—was 17% *white,* 62% Latino, and 21% Asian or African-American.

Yes: 83% of L.A.'s babies were *not* white. So why was this big, pretty ad on Sunset Boulevard so... *white!?* Did only white people drive down this strip of roadway, perhaps?

The executive set out to do a personal test the next day, amusing himself by returning to the billboard location by taking side streets that had only Spanish surnames—La Jolla, San Vicente, Santa Monica—which is to say, most any street in L.A. He sat with pen and paper in hand for twenty minutes and marked the demographics of each car that passed beneath the billboard.

Out of the 1,000 cars that he polled, 750 of the drivers were *not* white. This inspired the executive to dig down a bit deeper into the Fortune 500 firm that had created a billboard with such a diversity-oblivious ad. A Google search for the corporate name and "images" also brought up a field of white babies, each beautiful, each wearing the company's adorable clothes, and almost each one of the models being white. He did find a *few* Asian and African American babies mixed in, but, actually, not a single cute little Latino baby in the bunch.

Como es posible? he wondered. (Or, translated for the language impaired: "How is this possible?")

It is easy to find cute Latino babies in Los Angeles. And the language couldn't be a barrier to putting them in this ad. So why did a big company decide to target only 17% of the local population with its key images and marketing spend? How could they expect to remain an important brand to America's children, either now or when those kids became parents??

Hadn't this company noticed the success of the Walt Disney Company, the biggest brand in entertainment, when it aired its first-ever movie with a Latina princess in late 2012, *Sofia the First: Once Upon a Princess,* which became the highest rated cable telecast **of all time** for kids and girls age 2-5 and set a record for #1 preschool cable TV telecast for total viewers and adults 18-49**?!**[2] Or how they have now boldly introduced *Elena of Avalor,* the new Disney Channel series that features their company's first Latina princess and actively and "evocatively" represents Latin culture in its music, landscapes, and characters, because, as the show's Diane Rodriguez says, "(Latina girls) need their face reflected back to them."[3]

After his experiment and analysis, this executive went on to dream about putting up a new, competing billboard on Sunset Strip. One that was populated with babies of all races and ethnicities, along with the slogan, "Love ALL Your Customers at First Sight."[4]

###

Here's my question to you: Why isn't everyone selling that message today?

I have had the good fortune to be Chief Diversity & Inclusion Officer for a leading national non-profit sports association that is intensely committed to "loving our customers." We have undertaken the critical field research, soul-searching, and strategic planning process necessary to develop a comprehensive diversity & inclusion philosophy for our institution. We have read or met with leading thinkers and practitioners in this field. Out of that I have developed a framework that will permit you to use diversity and inclusion as a solid business strategy that builds not just your company, but its profit and influence, going forward.

Here is the indisputable reality for executives and corporations today: *if you are an executive and know how to operate in a diverse landscape, you will have a leg up on your competition for any C-Suite position. This practical "Big Six" strategy will guide you to success in developing a D&I action plan—your own Inclusion Solution— whether you work in corporate America, at a non-governmental organization (NGO), or lead an association or organization.*

I believe that most savvy executives today are attuned already to the diversity of the contemporary U.S. marketplace, but with this book I want to equip you, first, with all of the most current data and facts regarding American ethnic and racial diversity as it pertains to your product or service. In the event that you need to make a case or want to apply your institutional metrics to emerging national statistics, the first chapter will outline the "**New Normal**": where we are, and what we can expect from the marketing implications of 21st-century demographics.

The case that I make for diversity and inclusion is not just sociological or democratic: it is a **business strategy.** That is the focus of this book. That is how I developed the framework that I recommend for corporations and associations. I believe that you will find a way to increase your revenues directly through understanding the pathways that I provide here, and by implementing the **Big Six**

Action Plan that I outline, so that you can take a comprehensive and holistic business approach to diversity & inclusion in your own company. I will explain how you ensure a diverse workforce at every level, how you reach a multi-cultural marketplace, and how you include diversity in your image as a way of ensuring the greatest opportunities for growth and expansion.

Ultimately, diversity and inclusion should become part of your competitive advantage. You should make it a cornerstone to your strategy for achieving all of your organizational or corporate goals and objectives. You will find few strategies that bolster your bottom line in a more significant or enduring way.

Let me show you how.

CHAPTER 1

THE NEW NORMAL

NOT SO LONG AGO, while the United States as a country recognized that it was comprised of a melting pot of cultures and ethnicities, corporate America considered white male Anglo-Saxons to be the majority culture. When you're the majority culture, you come to define yourself, your views, and priorities as "normal." But, then, where does that leave everyone else? Well... you get the point.

The rapid demographic changes in the last ten years and looking forward to 2020 have distinctly redefined our understanding of the term "majority culture." It already no longer looks like it used to look. So we are in the process of aggressively reframing what we mean by "normal."

The demographic reality of the U.S. is this: 70% percent of the U.S. workforce is already comprised of women and/or African-Americans and Latinos.[5] That's before looking again at those customers. Your marketplace is being defined by the fact that, for the first time in U.S. history, less than half of all newborns in America are non-Hispanic Caucasian. The percentage of Americans who are white (non-Hispanic) is on a demographic trend downwards, particularly among our younger citizens. By 2050, according to the U.S. Census data, people of color will constitute the majority of our population.[6] This demographic shift is already showing its impact on our politics and economy.

So, as you can imagine, anyone who fails to fully embrace the "**New Normal**" of these changing demographics will also fail to capitalize on the substantial growth in buying power that these diverse markets represent. Not only are these diverse minority groups increasing as a percentage of the U.S. population, but so too is the buying power that they wield.

Currently, African-Americans are the largest minority among adults over 50 according to William H. Frey, a demographer at the Brookings Institution; by 2050, the Hispanics in this age group will comprise nearly 20% of the population.[7] But for the under-50 crowd—including those babies I mentioned earlier, who are making up our first "majority minority" generation—Latinos comprise the largest demographic group after non-white Europeans.

As of the 2014 Census report, 62.2% of the population is White, a number that falls to 43.6% over the next forty years. As of July 2015, there were more minority kids under the age of 5 than there were whites.[8] Our future!

37.8% of our population is "minority": 17.4% is Latino, 12.4% is African American, 5.2% is Asian American, 2% identify as members of two or more ethnic or racial minorities, and 1% are members of other ethnicities. And don't forget the fact that we also have over 42 million immigrants here currently, representing additional diverse perspectives within the U.S.

"It's a major turning point for American society," says Mr. Frey. "We're moving from a largely white and black population to one which is much more diverse and is a big contrast from what most baby boomers grew up with."[9] As he continued at the 2015 American Forum series, "We're about to encounter a diversity boom that's going to have as big of an impact, if not bigger, on this country than the baby boom in the second half of the last century... The reason is ... we have a huge growth in what I call new minorities: Hispanics, Asians, Multiracial Americans. In forty years, they're going to double in size. They already account for most of the growth in the United States and that's going to be huge."[10]

Our burgeoning diversity in the United States is no longer about immigration. The white component of our population is aging, and, compared to a few years ago, they are having fewer children to a much higher degree than parents of any other ethnic or racial group.

States like California and New Mexico, Hawaii and Texas are already majority minority (61.5% and 61.1%, 77% and 56.5% respectively). Summer 2015 estimates list the next states likely to surpass this threshold are Nevada (48.5 percent minority), Maryland (47.4 percent minority) and Georgia (45.7 percent minority), with states like New Jersey and Arizona next in line. Cities like the New York metropolitan area are 65% Latino, Black and Asian; the Los

Angeles area is 70.6% minority, the District of Columbia is 64.2%, Houston is 60%, and Miami-Ft. Lauderdale is 65%. A Pew map shows that, between 2000 and 2013, whites became the minority in 78 U.S. counties.[11] And the most populous county in America is majority minority, L.A. county—home to that white baby-clothes billboard.[12]

So, this **New Normal** is destined to generate numerous problems if you and your company do not have a comprehensive strategy for diversity and inclusion. I'll discuss the ramifications of this data in more depth in Chapter 2, but the bottom line is that any company, organization, or management unit that thinks the Old Normal is the Still Normal is destined to suffer seriously negative impacts on their bottom line. They will be beaten by any competitor who has embraced and incorporated the **New Normal** into key aspects of their business, from staffing and customer relations, to marketing and supplier alliances.

The first strategy for rooting out subtle bias and bigotry is the development of a deep understanding of the **New Normal.** This is essential. We can no longer use the former Caucasian mainstream as our benchmark for quality, competence, or "club membership." We can't evaluate non-white executive candidates with surprise that they're "so articulate." We can't use Human Resources (HR) phrases like "more than just the normal applicants." We need to identify where vestiges of the Old Normal remain in our thinking, policies, and interactions.

General Mills's unit director of Wellness Snacks, Carla Vernón, once learned from her advertising agency that they planned to feature a scientist and an assistant in their next ad. The agency planned to cast only Caucasian actors, because, "in a 30-second spot, the audience needs familiar archetypes for immediate understanding."

Clearly, General Mills's agency creative director was not aware that his client was both Latina and African-American and that her mother had a PhD in microbiology! His Old Normal mentality had to be replaced; otherwise, his agency was destined to lose an enormous contract.

"It's not about business inclusion because it's beautiful," Vernón said after the casting for her spot was amended. "Studies show that the best business results come from diverse agencies. You better scramble to get to the table."[13]

After working through this book, you and your company will no longer need to scramble. You will be well positioned at the table to increase profitability and cohesion. You probably have all of the **New Normal** data that you need already, but before I continue into the business argument, let me equip you with some additional information.

Women

You are most likely aware that American women outnumber men by nearly 5 million (162 v. 157 million; July 2015), that there are 132 women for every 100 men over age 65 and twice as many women than men over age 85. While 61.7% of women in the U.S. in 2015 were white, only 47.5 will be by 2050. The remainders are Latina (17.1%), African American (12.7%), Asian American (5.5%), Native American and Pacific Islander.

In the next ten years, the percentage of Hispanic women in the workforce is projected to increase 30.3%; of Asian women, 24.3%; and of African American women, 11.3%; while the percentage of white women in the labor force is expected to drop 2.1%.[14]

The other notable statistics about women that impact your diversity and inclusion strategy pertain to income and education. Women now outnumber men in college and graduate school; moreover, the education pattern of young workers makes it clear that women will soon be the majority of college-educated workers. In 2014, women ages 25 to 34 were more than twenty percent more likely than men to be college graduates.[15]

In 2013, in a sharp upward trend, the percentage of American wives who earn more than their husbands surpassed 33.5%; the U.S. Census Bureau also reports an incremental growth in the median annual earning of women older than 15 each year, to $39.621 in 2014[16], and $51,792 median income for executive and professional women in 2015.[17]

Women remain responsible for 85% of all consumer purchases, hold 89% of U.S. bank accounts, and women age 50 and older control net worth of $19 trillion and own over 75% of all personal wealth.[18] 80% of Pinterest users are women: is your brand there??[19] The marked increase in female members of Congress and the Senate at the 2012 and 2014 elections, as well as in state political leadership, indicates an anticipated significant expansion of women's political power by 2020, as well.

Those purchases that American women control represent $5-15 trillion annually in consumer and business spending.[20] Yet only 3% of advertising agency creative directors are women.[21] Isn't that incredible? No wonder women believe that advertisers and marketers don't "get" them!

African Americans

Blacks comprise 13.6% of the U.S. population, according to the 2010 Census and are projected to constitute 15% by 2050. The largest demographic block is 10-19 years old, closely followed by kids under age 9. That said, according to DiversityInc.com and the EEOC, only 4.9% of U.S. corporate managers and 2.9% of senior managers are Black. That, despite the fact that the percentage of African Americans with a bachelor's degree or higher has increased to 22.4%, and the number of the group's 25-29-year-olds with a high school education is over 91.9% in 2014.

Five Fortune 500 companies have Black CEOs (1%), 7.4% have African Americans on their Board of Directors, and the United States does have a Black Commander in Chief until the end of 2016. But you must agree: that is hardly enough Black top corporate leadership. The fact is that African American buying power is estimated to increase nearly 25% between now and 2019, and equal $1.6 trillion by 2018[22] 2/3 of Blacks shop online, they watch more TV than any other group, and their Internet use has more than doubled in the past ten years.[23]

This racial group's spending patterns are different than that of other minorities (e.g., more on footwear, children's clothing and phone services; less on dining out, health care, and vehicle purchases; they are larger patrons of beauty supply and convenience-oriented stores than other shoppers), and should be carefully analyzed and understood. There is rarely a better way to do so than through the inclusion of African American executives and senior staff in product development and marketing decisions.

Latinos/U.S. Hispanics

In 2015, Latinos represent over $1.3 trillion of buying power in the United States, larger than the GDP of Mexico, and climbs annually, consistently representing consumer spending greater than the entire economies of all but 13 countries in the world.[24] Driving this economic activity is the growth of the Hispanic population, what *Forbes Magazine* calls "far and away the most significant demographic trend reshaping America."[25] There are now 55.4 million Americans of Latin-American descent. By 2060 that number is projected to reach 128.8 million.[26] 55.2% of U.S. population growth over the past decade has come from this group.[27] If Hispanic Americans were a nation, it would have the world's eleventh-largest economy!

Today, 1 in every 6 Americans is Hispanic; by 2050, the ratio will be nearly 1 in 3. Hispanic households are larger than non-Hispanic (3.3 people v. 2.4, on average) and have twice as many members younger than 18. 65% of U.S. Latinos are members of the Millennial Generation, aged 22-35, the very most desirable market for goods, services, and entertainment.[28] Most big consumer products companies are finding that the bulk of their growth comes from increased demand from Latino customers. So Trujillo, former CEO of USWest, France's Orange SA, and Australia's Telstra Corp., has served on Target's board and said that he's familiar with situations where 75% or more of consumer-facing companies' revenue growth comes from the Latino market.[29]

"The Hispanic market is no longer being viewed as a niche, minority market for a lot of companies," says Alex Ruelas, cofounder of the Austin-based-marketing agency LatinWorks. "It's becoming a fairly major part of the mainstream, and it's helping to reshape the overall universe of consumers in a way that's a bit surprising to people."[30]

So, as Ruelas goes on to explain, if you are designing a marketing plan for a huge company like Pepsi Co. or Procter & Gamble, or if you are developing membership services and outreach for a national organization, you must recognize how critical it is to understand the Hispanic market because, even though they may still have a slightly lower than average household income, Latinos are more frequent shoppers in supercenters, mass merchandisers and drugstores and buy many products—from staples and   electronics to baby-related goods and soft drinks—far more frequently than any other demographic segment.

Remember: the median age of U.S. Latinos is 27 years old. Of non-Hispanic white people? 42 years old!! These particular market members are still developing their brand preferences, have disposable income, tend to be trend setters, and... are hard to reach through the channels developed for the "Old Normal."[31] Some companies are also becoming very astute in their design of marketing distinctions for the different nationalities of origin that make up the Hispanic market. 64.6% are Mexican, for example, 9.5% are Puerto Rican, and the Cuban, Salvadoran, and Dominican communities are expanding each year.

Other companies tackle the Latino market head on. Why do we celebrate Cinco de Mayo, instead of Mexico's true Independence Day in September? Because Coors Brewing Company, which had been boycotted by Chicano activists for Latino labor discrimination, signed agreements with leading Hispanic civil rights groups, then used their good will to pour marketing dollars into encouraging college students to drink more beer in May![32] National Hispanic Heritage Month, September 15—October 15, is another key marketing and programming opportunity for this community.

22% of kids under age 18 are Latino. 15% of college enrollment in 2012 was Latino and rising. High school and college education percentages increase each year; 15.1% have at least a Bachelor's degree and over 66% have completed high school. More than half (55%) of Latinos live in California, Texas, and Florida; many counties and states across the nation experienced dramatic rises in their Latino populations over the last ten years, as reported in the 2010 Census.[33] The Hispanic share of purchasing power has increased in every state since 2000, and is projected to continue to do so.

This is not just about population and consumption metrics. As Dan Holly, editor of *Diversity MBA* found himself "shocked" to discover, as noted in a May 2016 article, "Hispanic-owned businesses are growing at a rate 15 times the national average, according to a recent report jointly conducted by the research firm GEOSCAPE and the U.S. Hispanic Chamber of Commerce ... Why are Hispanics jumping at the opportunity to create new businesses like it's the gold rush of the 1800s?

"What it tells me is that the people who are most familiar with the Hispanic market see great opportunity. It tells that the people most familiar with the Hispanic market feel that Hispanic consumers are underserved by the business world ... As much as businesses big and small are courting the Hispanic consumer, that number—15 times the national average—suggests there is room to go **farther.**" [34]

A recent issue of *Diversity MBA Magazine* had an article about a Latino who worked his way up the ladder to become CEO of a New York City bank, one of the country's oldest lending institutions with a rich history, steeped in tradition. As Holly summarized, after the banker "embraced his Hispanic roots" to help the institution where he worked, the bank is thriving and nearly fifty percent of its new customers are Hispanic.

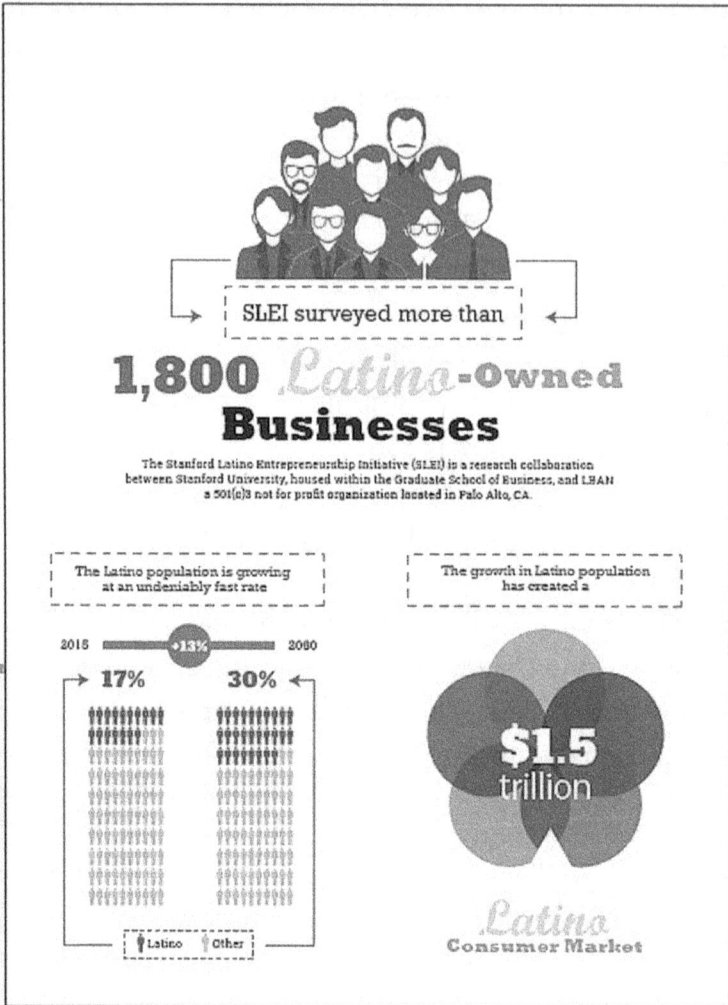

Forbes's Latino Entrepreneurs Chart[35]

Language is the big issue of debate in marketing and diversity circles, as more Hispanic children are born in the U.S. and bilingual household members use Spanish to cross generations more than for professional or entertainment pursuits. But Spanglish has made its mark on the cable and advertising landscape, with more of it expected in the future as a way to speak directly to the Hispanic-American experience.

Asian Americans & Pacific Islanders

While this minority comprises only 5.6% of the total U.S. population, according to the 2010 Census, the Asian/Pacific Islander population grew 46% between 2000 and 2010, more than any other racial group. Like Latinos, the Asian community grew and spread beyond their traditional states and cities during the course of the past decade; they showed the most population growth in Nevada, Arizona, North Carolina, Georgia, and New Hampshire.

The U.S. Census Bureau includes citizens of numerous origins among this group: Chinese comprise 3.3 million, Asian Indians are 2.8 million, Filipinos 2.5 million, Koreans 1.5 million, Vietnamese 1.6 million, and Japanese nearly 775,000 in 2010.

This is a highly educated and professionalized demographic. 50% of all Asian Americans have Bachelor's degrees compared with 25% of all Americans; 20% have advanced degrees compared with a national average of 10%. Asian buying power increased nearly 37% between 2009 and 2014, just slightly faster than Latinos', and should reach $1 trillion by 2017. The 2012 median weekly income for Asians, at $918, is higher than any other group's including whites ($793). The Asian life expectancy, at 85.8 years, is the highest of any ethnic or racial minority.[36]

Asian Americans are avid consumers of media, including print, and prefer their ads presented in their own languages. Over 120 magazines targeting specific Asian countries of origin are published in the U.S., and Asians read more women's, business & finance, news weeklies, general editorial magazines and home service publications than any other group of Americans.[37]

LGBTQIA

Gay marriage has been upheld before the Supreme Court. Active sports professionals are coming out for the first time. Intersex children are being permitted to transition in middle school, and a group of experts from 21 federal agencies has been tasked for a project to figure out how to collect data on the nation's LGBT population and how they live "for a host of legal, economic and medical reasons."[38] Although 92% of organizations surveyed in late 2015 track diversity according to gender (and 88% by ethnicity, race, or 85% by age), only 31% are measuring the diversity of their employee demographics by sexual orientation and 28% by gender identity, but more and more these are critical D&I metrics that pertain to various aspects of your mission, talent, and audience or service community.[39] Inclusion and diversity now definitively umbrella issues that pertain to gender and sexual identity.

Lesbian is a female-identified person who is attracted romantically, physically, or emotionally to another female-identified person. Gay refers to a male-identified person attracted romantically, physically, or emotionally to another male-identified person. Bisexual is a person who is attracted romantically, physically, or emotionally to both men and women. Transgender is someone who identifies as a gender other than that expected, based on anatomical sex. Queer is an umbrella term that embraces the variety of sexual preferences, orientations, and habits of people who don't adhere to the heterosexual and cisgender (gender aligns with anatomical sex) majority, including but not limited to lesbians, gay men, bisexuals, trans people, and intersex persons. Intersex is someone whose physical sex characteristics aren't categorized as exclusively male or female. Asexual is a person without attractions or sexual orientation. And an ally is someone who doesn't identify as LGBTQIA, but who supports the rights and safety of those who do.[40]

3.8% of Americans identify as LGBT, or more than 8.5 million people, and 6% of gay or lesbian parents are raising adopted or biological children.[41] Same-sex married and unmarried couples have an average household income of $115,000 and $110,223, respectively, while married opposite-sex households average $101,487, and unmarried opposite-sex couples' households, $69,511.[42] The median household income for gay male couples is $130,000.[43]

The LGBT community is estimated to control buying power of over $800 billion annually, is more likely to pay for quality brands, to influence others, and to remain intensely loyal to brands that provide equal workplace benefits (81%) and that support causes relevant to them (74%).[44] 71% of the LGBT community has a college or graduate school education, 86-87% vote, and "LGBT friendly" is evaluated in terms of states and cities where gay and lesbian families buy homes and bring business.

As former RBC Wealth Management CEO John Taft explained to *Affinity Inc Magazine,* (before he retired in May 2016), RBC "is committed to ensuring that its employees understand the needs of the LGBT community through advisor training.

"'In 2015, we launched a marketing campaign containing information and tools for advisors to work with same-sex couples, managing wealth and setting up estate plans," Taft said. 'There is a lot of activity in that space, as LGBT couples get married and take advantage of the same benefits and structuring opportunities that heterosexual couples have had for years.'

"RBC is also committed to diversifying its own employee based by attracting and retaining LGBT employees. For five years, RBC Wealth Management-U.S. has earned 100 percent ratings from the Human Rights Campaign in its Corporate Equality Index as one of the Best Places to Work for LGBT Equality, evidence of the company's commitment to supporting its diverse employee base and inclusive culture."[45]

Seniors

The Boomers have reached age 65: they're Seniors and number over 46 million people in the United States, alone. It's a faster growing demographic than the population under age now 45. 1 in every 7 Americans (14.5%) is 65 years old or older.[46] By 2060, given longer lifespans and lower birthrates, Pew Research Center projects that there will be almost as many Americans over the age of 85 as there will be under age 5.[47] Just as the "New Normal" of the United States is becoming progressively majority minority or non-white, so is it becoming swiftly more "gray."

Plans for inclusion of this population segment may pertain more to marketing and service strategies than employment and recruitment, but should recognize the distinct needs and economic capacity of the many American Seniors. Minorities account for 21.2% of this group, and will increase to 21.1 million, or 28.5% by 2030, so diversity will play an added role in any plan for this demographic, as well.[48]

While 90% of Seniors receive Social Security (SS) benefits, and median incomes are low, just the $849 billion in 2014 SS benefits alone account for a sizable market, let alone the personal retirement wealth of this population.[49] Current estimates on Seniors' access to resources pegs it at $20 trillion, with $1.6 trillion in annual spending power.[50] Leisure time is so much greater in this than any other demographic that it is a key market target, in addition to health care, food, housing and transportation.

The Disabled

There are 57 million disabled people in the United States. Since the adoption twenty-five years ago of the American Disabilities Act (ADA), many things have improved for this segment of our population, but employment is not one of them. In fact, according to CNN Money, employment for disabled Americans has decreased since 1990, and "there's an even bigger gap between disabled and non-disabled jobs prospects today."[51]

Reversing these statistics and finding meaningful inclusion for this portion of our population has involved a change in policies and trainings by individual companies plus a commitment to making technological innovations that can remove barriers to participation by disabled applicants, employees, or consumers.

According to Susan Dooha, executive director of the Center for Independence of the Disabled, as companies, organizations, and institutions begin to include disability as an element of diversity, they will start to reverse "the thinking that they are a burden and instead (think) about them as having strength to bring to the workforce."[52]

Millennials

Generations of loosely twenty years in length tend to experience the same sets of historical events and share what the Pew Research Center calls a "generational persona."[53] They grow up and move as a unique demographic block, and they react in their own ways to the specific generations that come before and after them.

While seniors are a demographic unit of significance, so is our rising young adult generation, if only because, due to the wave of Asian-American and Hispanic-American children born to recent immigrants, this is the most racially and ethnically diverse generation our country has known.[54] More than four in ten are non-white, and as a cohort, or generation, they have unique characteristics different from all others before or since.

As Pew's *The Next Generation* report describes, they're political and social liberals, social media wizards, highly educated, slow to marry, and not very religious. They over-index in both low-paying jobs and high levels of college debt, which explains why a significant proportion "boomerang" to live back home with parents at some point.[55] Nevertheless, despite the challenges of the U.S. economy these past eight to ten years, when many of them began to launch into jobs and careers, this is considered a highly optimistic group, as well.

A 2015 study by Deloitte and the Billie Jean King Leadership Initiative (BJKLI) found that Millennials define and view diversity in different terms than other generations. They see diversity as "the blending of different backgrounds, experiences, and perspectives within a team, which is known as cognitive diversity," and considered by them to be a "necessary element for innovation" and look at diversity as "the combination of these unique traits to overcome challenges and achieve business goals."[56]

While the Baby Boom and GenX generations define diversity as "a representation of fairness and protection to all, regardless of gender, race, religion, ethnicity, or sexual orientation," and inclusion as "the business environment that integrates individuals of all of the above demographics into one workplace," through their unique lens, Millennials see inclusion as "the support for a collaborative environment that values open participation from individuals with different ideas and perspectives that has a positive impact on business."[57]

Their impact is enormous for employers and sellers of products and services. They are also becoming the drivers of our political system, albeit slowly. The 2015 decisions in favor of gay marriage and expanded rights for the LGBTQ communities, for example, can be tied to the social views and advocacy of Millennials in particular. In the year before the Supreme Court decision, 68% of Millennials favored the legalization, and that percentage has increased since then. Contrast that with 48% of Baby Boomers, ahead of the final determination, and 38% of the older, "Silent Generation."[58]

Generation Z

According to a new CBS News analysis, the newest generation in our demographics, at 60 million strong and a quarter of the U.S. population, already outnumbers Millennials by over a million members! And since, according to the 2010 U.S. Census data, our Hispanic population rose over 27.3 million people in the prior ten years and the number of Americans identifying as black-and-white and Asian-and-white mixed race biracial "rose by 134% and 87% respectively," our Generation Z is also even more—much more!—diverse than those before it.[59]

This is the population segment born between 1995 and 2010, sometimes known as "the Centennials." Although the youngest members have yet to enter elementary school, already this demographic group has a personality based on shared experiences of world events during their brief lifetime, a direction for growth and, according to J. Walter Thompson, annual purchasing power in the U.S. already of $44 billion![60]

Because of the social, economic, and political events of their years on Earth, already these young people are considered "more pragmatic" and diverse than Millennials. CBS makes the comparison to the Silent Generation (born mid-1920s to early 1940s), whose members also grew up during economic recession/depression and with the impacts of war. In the way those men and women became "diligent and pragmatic careerists, primarily averse to taking idealistic risks," so too may today's young people develop a much less optimistic and even more conservative bent, compared to the generation that precedes them.[61]

While the digital revolution occurred as Millennials grew up, members of Generation Z are "history's first generation of digital natives." They don't learn or adjust to the online space; "it's all they've ever known," whether for communication, social interaction, or acquisition of knowledge and information.[62] They are even more cautious and private than Millennials, having learned from their predecessors' mistakes in the social media environment. But so are their attention spans even shorter and their demands of marketing and communication more exacting.

Generation Z may be growing up with an equal measure of challenges and magnificent advances, but like generations before them, they will likely overcome some of their native "world-weariness" and become an impressive economic force to be reckoned with. After all, as CBS News reminds us, the Silent Generation was the richest generation in history.[63]

###

Diversity is about what makes each of us unique. It includes our backgrounds, personality, life experiences, and beliefs: all of the things that make us who we are. It is a combination of the visible and invisible differences that shape our view of the world, our perspective and our approach.

Age, gender, and sexual orientation, race, ethnicity and cultural perspective, even physical abilities account for different dimensions of diversity that should be examined by your inclusion plan. Your employees and suppliers represent a diverse population. So do your buyers, clients, and service community. Developing a strategy for the **New Normal** is critical for any company or organization in America right now.

Why?

Because it makes absolutely solid business sense.

COMPANY CASE STUDY
Approaches to Diversity: Intel & Pinterest

After revelations by Silicon Valley's top technology companies that their statistics for employee diversity and inclusion were poor for women and minorities, many of those industry leaders began to hack the problem and find solutions that would bring greater access and representation across all job positions and departments.

Intel and Pinterest have demonstrated tremendous leadership in their approach to 21st-century recruitment and training, retention and integration, starting with social media leader Pinterest's hiring Candice Morgan in January 2016 as their first-ever Chief Diversity Officer.

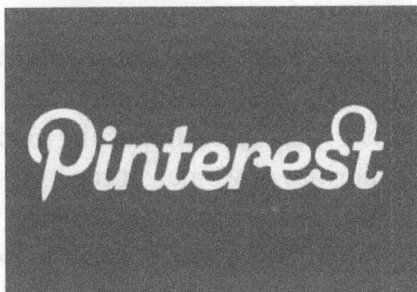

One place where Pinterest began their diversity and inclusion efforts, once they did a thorough internal analysis, was in sharing the problem openly and honestly. They used the reporting of their internal metrics as a way to introduce new, comprehensive targets for bringing women and minorities into the company and for supporting, training, retaining, and advancing those already in the Pinterest fold.

Intel CEO Brian Krzanich rolls out the company's new diversity initiatives at the 2015 Consumer Electronics Show
(via Engadget/Richard Lai)

Another tech giant that added D&I priorities companywide was Intel, whose Director of Global Employee Communications & Diversity Rosalind Hudnell revealed a $300 million program to achieve "full representation" of women and minorities in its U.S. workforce by 2020.

Traditionally, one of Intel's best sources for recruitment has been employee referrals. But in summer 2015, the company recognized that these were not supporting their ambitions to attract veterans, minorities or women at the levels they needed to meet their D&I goals. So the company decided to double their referral bonus for any employee who brought to the company new hires in their target demographics. Yes, they believe in diversity enough to guarantee $4,000 for each successful referral to Intel!

CHAPTER 2

BUSINESS CASE:
Why Diversity & Inclusion?

HERE IS WHAT IS CLEAR right from the start: if you do not have equitable engagement with the many different demographic groups that make up the United States, along with a well-developed diversity & inclusion strategy for your corporation or organization, you are destined for a slew of problems that no manager wants to navigate. A deficiency in diversity and inclusion will lead any business or association to experience unequal retention, regrettable loss, sub-optimized productivity, and low innovation. Any executive who is deficient in diversity & inclusion management skills is sure to be beaten by a competitor who has them. Furthermore, Business-to-Business companies really must have diversity efforts in place, if they plan to sell to progressive companies. Request-For-Proposals (RFPs) now include questions about diversity and supplier diversity over 90% of the time. You should also be aware that a lack of diversity & inclusion efforts can expose your company to potential liabilities from lawsuits.

As Deloitte affirmed in their "Reaffirming the Business Case for Diversity" in late 2011, "there is a robust business case for diversity, but the details are not quite captured by the headlines. The case rests on understanding that diversity means more than having a sprinkle of women and a dab of colour, and that the value of diversity lies in developing an inclusive workplace--and that means adaptation, not just assimilation and tolerance."[64] In a 2011 Forbes Insight survey of 300 multi-national executives, 41% identified the *"failure to perceive the connection between diversity and business drivers"* as a barrier to developing and implementing a diversity strategy that would help any company meet its bottom-line objectives.

The business case for diversity actually has two components. One is your bottom line and how your company's balance sheet will reflect any successful plan for diversity and inclusion. The second element, however, is "the heart of the matter." In the twenty-first century, companies and institutions are expected to contribute returns both to their shareholders *and* to society.[65] Organizations that reflect diverse values are now destined to greater success.

Because, in our country, people of color will soon represent the majority, our corporations now have a chance to expand their product and service offerings to myriad new markets and demographic groups. At the core of what has proven to be successful in these efforts, however, is "an authentic understanding of the audience and a commitment to investing in their communities."[66] The benefits of really mastering diversity and inclusion, as I will show you in the next chapters, are that not only will you contribute to your company's bottom line, but you will enhance your brand awareness and reputation, as well.

As Chubb Insurance USA confirms, "in order for Chubb to remain competitive for talent and for customers, it is imperative that we attract and value diverse talent and enable that talent to attract and value diverse customers." That seems clear. Companies have always needed to attract and retain the best workers, the necessary skills, and essential resources. The key to that now, however, is *diversity*. Given the demographics that I described in the **New Normal** chapter, plus advances in technology, communications, and globalization, diversity *is* your key driver of corporate growth.

Diversity is about acknowledging and leveraging similarities and differences as well as increased creativity and innovation, recruitment and retention of top talent, access to a changed marketplace, enabling people to unlock their potential so that they achieve their aspirations, how you lead teams, and, ultimately, your ability to leverage your resources to outperform your competitors. In addition, diversity *also* has a social component. It involves *inclusion* and *respect*. As you implement a solid inclusion framework and increase your capabilities through diversity, your business will change the way that it works with anyone who has different experiences or backgrounds. You will become more receptive to different ideas, and you will know that you're doing the right thing.[67]

Korn Ferry senior partner in workforce performance, diversity and inclusion practice Andrés Tapia says, "It's a good start when company leadership realizes, 'We're not diverse! Let's be diverse! Let's reflect the world!' That's great— that passion and excitement is needed—but in our approach with clients, the key question is always, how are you going to grow profitability?

"Through these talks, CEOs come to understand that many more of their business strategies than they realized can be accomplished by having a truly diverse workforce, especially because it enables them to reach new markets. So many CEOs are well intentioned when it comes to diversity, but they've truly missed the boat by only tangentially tying diversity to business. We must go beyond diversity just being a talent issue; it's truly a business issue."[68]

Diversity and inclusion are clearly the right things to do, and as I illuminate throughout these pages, they can deliver substantial contributions to your business efforts.

COMPANY CASE STUDY

Approach to Diversity: General Mills

General Mills made a significant commitment to diversity and inclusion at all levels of the company. In 2013, they ensured that 26% of new hire were workers of color. They also brought diversity to their C-suite positions and corporate governance. There are two prominent African American executives on General Mills's thirteen-person board of directors, the body responsible for providing oversight of the company's corporate performance and policy. The company also has a twenty-member senior management team, which includes three African Americans members.

One of the keys to General Mills putting their D&I policies into practices is the implementation of a diversity scorecard (described in depth in Chapter 5). Senior managers at the company use it to establish annual goals for attaining diversity in all departments and positions. They also incorporate an incentive structure for attaining benchmarks and targets.

Black Enterprise Magazine reports that General Mills' Chairman and CEO Kendall Powell "approves all senior officers' diversity objectives, and top managers work with diversity liaisons to create opportunities within certain departments." [69]

One program unique to the company and linked to their D&I success is the Black Champions Network, which identifies and promotes African American talent within the company, including professional development and support executive advancement. General Mills also organizes an annual Development and Leadership Day, complete with mentorship programs that position new minority hires for long-term success.

The business case for diversity goes hand in hand with inclusion, which involves the ways in which a company or association value and include any and all individuals. Part of any successful diversity strategy that brings success to your business must involve inclusive leadership that ensures that all of your employees have the opportunity to fulfill their potential and bring to their jobs all that they have to offer.

According to Miller and Katz (2002): "Inclusion increases the total human energy available to an organization. People can bring far more of themselves to their jobs because they are required to suppress far less."[70] As Deloitte reminds us, you can have a diverse workforce without inclusion; and inclusion without diversity. But one without the other is only half of the business performance equation. "Put simply: diversity + inclusion = improved business outcomes."[71]

Catalyst published a lot of recent data regarding the actual business facts and figures related to diversity. Their 2011 report, for example, which looks at women on boards of directors at Fortune 500 companies, found "better financial performance on average (in terms of return on sales, return on invested capital, and return on equity) than those with the lowest representation of women.[72] Top-listed European companies with gender diversity in management achieved higher than average stock performance—64% versus 47%.[73]

The McKinsey & Company *Women Matter* report series had similar findings when it analyzed companies across

Europe, Brazil, Russia, India and China in 2010; that report showed that companies with the highest share of women in their senior management teams outperformed those with no women by 41% in terms of return on equity (22% vs. 15%) and by 56% in terms of operating results (17% vs. 11%).

Another study, done by Professor Cedric Herring at the University of Illinois at Chicago based on research of 506 U.S. organizations, also showed that those with greater racial and gender diversity performed better in terms of sales revenues, number of customers, and market share.[74] Workplace diversity is among the most important predictors of a business' sales revenue, customer numbers, and profitability, according to his research, which was published in the April 2009 issue of the *American Sociological Review*. "For example, a one unit increase in racial diversity increased the number of customers by more than 400, and 200 for gender diversity; and a one unit increase in racial diversity increased sales revenue by 9%, and 3% for gender diversity."[75]

However, as PricewaterhouseCoopers reported in October 2015, nearly ninety percent of the executives who set on boards are white, only thirty-five percent of male directors said gender diversity was "very important" and only thirty-one percent of male board members said diversity improves company performance. FHW Squared president/CEO Dr. Christopher Metzler insists that board diversity is "something worth fighting for. It can lead to more accurate governance. Diverse people with contrasting experiences and points of view on governance, engaging customers and delivering on a company's brand promise help the board make better decisions ... A balanced board will have more representatives of its products, users and customers to help make more informed decisions. It may be especially important for consumer-facing industries to have female directors, and for multinational companies to include foreign nationals on a board. ... Having a heterogeneous board can also enhance an organization's reputation. ... These days, more institutional investors take board diversity into account as a factor for investment evaluation because of the various academic research papers that indicate a positive correlation between firm value and board diversity, and institutional investors are placing greater emphasis on corporate social responsibility."[76]

This is not to say that the success of your D&I efforts will be a foregone conclusion. To realize the success pointed in these metrics takes an active approach that examines many levels of your business strategies. As global D&I thought leader Andrés Tapia says to CEOs on a regular basis, "Don't just say you're a champion of diversity. You need cross-cultural agility. You need to be honest with yourself and have the self-awareness to understand that the system in place is actually averse to attracting diverse people. It's really just time to change the system."[77]

Let me introduce you to my approach to Diversity and Inclusion, and the 6-part strategic direction that can lead you to similar success.

COMPANY CASE STUDY

Approach to Diversity: Coca-Cola

One of the most comprehensive and sophisticated strategies for D&I was developed and implemented by The Coca-Cola Company. Led by former Chief Diversity Officer Steve Bucherati, it has been directly correlated to the company's business success on many fronts.

Creating and "selling" the various corporate initiatives was not without challenges. For example, The Coca-Cola Company launched a women's initiative under Bucherati's twenty-four years leadership of worldwide diversity initiatives. As he told *DiversityInc* about getting that off the ground, he was "well aware that he (is) one of only a handful of straight white men in the diversity field," but "he feels this enables him to relate to other white men in the corporate world." Around this specific initiative, he said about his primarily white, male colleagues in corporate leadership, "'my brand had value. I showed them that this is not an effort to invalidate them; it's an effort to validate everyone."'[78]

As a global leader in their product space, it has been significant that the company states boldly and openly, "Diversity is an integral part of who we are, how we operate and how we see the future. The Coca-Cola Company leverages a worldwide team that is rich in diverse people, talent and ideas. As a global business, our ability to understand, embrace and operate in a multicultural world— both in the marketplace and in the workplace—is critical to our sustainability."

Bucherati's efforts ranged from the top to bottom of his company, starting with supplier diversity. He developed a detailed D&I strategy that included long-term segmented marketing plans to reach consumers in a wide variety of racial and ethnic groups. The Coca-Cola Company became a leader in building signification relationships between their brand and prominent communities, events, and institutions of influence, and in giving back in ways that had important impact on diverse constituencies worldwide.

Their partners include the Adelante Movement for Latina entrepreneurs, Black History Month, the Chinese Lunar New Year, and Hispanic Heritage Month. They support multi-cultural scholarship and foundation efforts in education, media events like the Essence Festival and the BET Awards, and diverse sporting ventures like the Special Olympics and the FIFA World Cup.

And these diverse partnerships "give back" both to communities, customers, and stakeholders but also to the company's bottom line. A 2010 partnership initiative with Target developed specifically for Asian consumers in specific stores increased sales 180%.

In addition to Coca-Cola's Global Women's Initiative, the company has fifteen resource groups that include participation from over a third of their employees. New Chief Diversity Officer John Lewis continues the tradition of presenting participation and diversity progress to the company's board of directors as further evidence that D&I is a priority at the company's highest levels. As he said in his Coca-Cola Diversity Stewardship Report, "Today's diversity dialogue, as it was in Dr. Martin Luther King Jr.'s day, is about the forgotten, the silenced and the institutionally marginalized, and all that we collectively stand to lose by not bringing their talent, energy, perspective and passion to the marketplace."[79]

The dialogue and priorities continue at one of the world's largest and most successful companies with the most highly recognized brands.

CHAPTER 3

THE APPROACH

YOU WILL FINISH THIS BOOK ready to make diversity and inclusion a key business strategy for your company or association. The foundation of your own Inclusion Solution will follow the framework that I lay out in Chapter 4—the Big Six action plan. It will show you, point by point, how to formulate an approach that is unique to your organization, and which embeds diversity and inclusion into every aspect of your enterprise, from business culture to employee engagement and from market penetration to talent management.

First, however, you need to establish some key objectives that pertain specifically to your institution, corporation, or organization. Once you embrace the idea that diversity & inclusion can help you to sustain successful growth and create value for your shareholders or members, I recommend that you and your management *make diversity and inclusion a core value* of your corporation. It needs to be a stated commitment, like any other brand promise or mission statement.

Once diversity and inclusion are elevated to this level of focus and priority, then you will have erected the first tentpoles for D&I and taken the first steps to weave them into your institutional fabric. You are now able to commit that your corporate or management approach to every strategic mandate or plan will address diversity from that point forward. From this, you will be able to develop the tactics that ensure that you realize your D&I targets based on this core commitment. You will have defined those values that distinguish your company and guide your every action.

D&I Statement

Begin by *making Diversity and Inclusion a strategic priority f*or your corporation. Include this affirmation in your institutional business or strategic plan, and then drill down on the following levels of detail, in order to build the framework on which your tactics and strategies will be established.

Make D&I a core value of your brand, division, association, or corporation. Write a D&I Statement. In it, articulate exactly what flows from diversity and inclusion. Then be sure to post it on your website and in your employee and supplier materials.

There is some latitude to the crafting of a corporate or organizational Diversity Statement. Some of them are short; others are a few paragraphs long:

❖ In 2012, Steve Pemberton, Chief Diversity Officer at Walgreens and his D&I team secured senior leadership approval and sponsorship for a new comprehensive strategy to integrate diversity and inclusion into everything they do. Their Diversity and Inclusion Vision Statement is:

> *To be within the next three years, a "Next Practices" company for Diversity and Inclusion, whose cultures, people, perspectives and workplaces will reflect the current and future customers we serve while delivering superior business performance.*

❖ Angela L. Talton, Nielsen's Chief Diversity Officer, works with her CEO to weave diversity into every business aspect. Their statement is:

> *At Nielsen, diversity is not just a goal, it is a business imperative. Our effectiveness at embracing the talents of people of different backgrounds, experiences and perspectives is key to our continued success in providing clients with information they need to succeed, and in making certain that all communities and individuals we depend upon to provide us with information about consumer behavior understand who we are, what we do and agree to participate in our consumer samples.*

❖ Staples' chairman and CEO Ron Sargent offers this Diversity Statement, then goes on to explain in specifics how it is that they will accomplish it (see more on that in Chapter 4):

We've built a great company by embracing the differences of our associates, customers and the communities we serve. And our commitment to diversity will grow even stronger as we build the Staples of the future. Our goal is to reflect the faces of our customers in every market where Staples has a presence. Only then will we achieve our vision of being the world's best office products company.

❖ Erika Irish Brown, Global Head of Diversity & Inclusion, shares her company's Bloomberg L.P.'s diversity statement:

Bloomberg's diverse workforce and open culture are essential to innovation and the key to our success. Our efforts help establish an inclusive work environment where all Bloomberg employees feel respected for their diversity and empowered to impact the business globally.

❖ The McDonald's corporation's Global Chief Diversity Officer Patricia Harris articulates their diversity statement on the company's website and materials:

The heart of the McDonald's organization is in providing doorways of opportunities and growth for team members from diverse backgrounds and communities locally—and internationally. Respecting, listening to and participating in knowledge-sharing and eclectic insights has helped make us the organization we are today— from our crew members to our board members.

Others are more succinct. UCLA's Chancellor states that "diversity is a core value" of the University. Google "strives to create a wholly inclusive workplace everywhere we operate in the world" because "diversity is an essential component of the culture at Google," and something that they want to celebrate.

The USTA has a business scope within the United States, and a mission that, of course, focuses on the growth of tennis. A portion of the USTA's Diversity & Inclusion Statement states that "Diversity allows us to touch 'all of America' and inclusion allows 'all of America' to touch us."

Definitions

Within your company, organization, department, or work group, start by agreeing on the definitions of the words "diversity" and "inclusion." This need only be a sentence or two for each term, but once you do, it will be easier to understand how they then relate to your mission—not your *diversity* mission; your essential corporate or business mission.

Diversity may mean "a wide range of interests, backgrounds, experiences."

Or "differences among groups of people and individuals based on ethnicity, race, socioeconomic status, gender, exceptionalities, language, religion, sexual orientation, and geographical area."

Diversity may focus on human and institutional, viewpoints, backgrounds, and life experiences, on "tolerance of thought, ideas, people with differing viewpoints, backgrounds, and life experiences."

The variety reflected under the diversity umbrella does include different opinions, backgrounds (degrees and social experience), religious beliefs, political beliefs, sexual orientations, heritage, and life experience.

You need to decide.

And then do the same exploration and determination for the word inclusion. How is your company's specific environment designed to respect and encourage the kind of participation that will support your own business and social objectives?

Ernst & Young (EY; #3 on DiversityInc's 2016 Top 50 companies for diversity) and their Director, Global and Americas Diversity and Inclusion Diana Solash, have a firm statement of D&I embedded in their mission and purpose. They then articulate their own definitions in articulating their approach to diversity and inclusiveness:

"Our focus on diversity and inclusiveness is integral to how we serve our clients, develop our people and play a leadership role in our communities.

- **Diversity is about differences.** Each of us is different, and at EY we value and respect individual differences. At EY, we think broadly about differences; they include background, education, gender, ethnicity, nationality, generation, age, working and thinking styles, religious background, sexual orientation, ability and technical skills. There are also differences according to service line, sector and function.
- **Inclusiveness is about leveraging these differences to achieve better business results.** It is about creating an environment where all of our people feel, and are, valued, where they are able to bring their differences to work each day, and where they contribute their personal best in every encounter.

"Research shows that companies with diverse teams that are led inclusively perform better than those with more homogenous teams. Diverse teams are more likely to improve market share and have success in new markets; they demonstrate stronger collaboration and better retention.

"Making sure that all our people's voices are heard and valued not only helps attract and retain the best people, but it also helps us deliver better approaches for our clients and for our own organization. That is because creating an inclusive workforce, where **all** difference matter, allows us to identify the risks and opportunities we might not otherwise see."[80]

This is just one example but may serve as inspiration to your own definition development. Next, let's look at some Who/What/Whys.

WHY? Importance

Each company should **define why an effective diversity and inclusion strategy is critical** to achieving their own unique essential business purposes. This is something that can next be *stated*, as part of the initial parameters for building a comprehensive approach to D&I.

Are there top business directives or strategic directions that comprise your corporate plan? Acknowledge that your Diversity and Inclusion strategy is going to be integral to the success of each one of those initiatives or business goals.

Additionally, as I mentioned in Chapter 2, every organization has a corporate responsibility to create a respectful, inclusive work and commercial environment, one that requires management to take the lead in removing barriers to opportunity and diversity on every level of your business.

WHO? Target Audiences

It takes some analysis of your workforce, stakeholders, audience, and markets to identify the target audience for your diversity initiative. You can establish some "primary focus areas" around ethnic, racial, ability, or sexual orientation, for example. These would be specific and appropriate to your product, your mission, or the operations of your enterprise.

But, of course, you will want to acknowledge that all of the many components of diversity discussed in Chapter 1 (as well as many other dimensions of diversity) should be included in your thinking. You want to maximize the creativity and contributions that any employee, market, supplier, or stakeholder can make to your operations and business success.

Be inclusive!!

WHAT? D&I Philosophy

I hope that you can establish a Diversity and Inclusion department, business unit, or strategic team that will be charged to research, envision, and implement your ultimate D&I Plan of Attack throughout your company. Depending on the size of your organization and the structure of your management, this may become your unique purpose and that of a team dedicated to helping every facet of your corporation realize the strategic priority of diversity and inclusion.

Your business always has goals and objectives. Managers with D&I responsibilities at your company need to design a range of Diversity & Inclusion tools and solutions that meet the overall corporate ambitions. Your "customers," as a D&I executive, may be the market to which you sell products, but they may also be the various product development, HR, and marketing departments within your corporation.

What I'm going to offer you, as the ***Big Six*** elements of your Strategic Direction, will help you to develop an action plan that works for your "customers." But first, state your D&I philosophy—whether for your job, your department, or your company, at large.

Then dive in and lay a foundation for creating a Strategic Direction that applies specifically to implementing D&I best practices throughout your enterprise.

COMPANY CASE STUDY
Approach to Diversity: EMC Corp. & Starbucks

As valued transgender employees continue to join our diverse employee ranks and as their unique social, political, and medical needs become part of our core HR values, corporate America has begun to respond to their visibility and their benefit needs in exemplary ways.

According to Human Rights Campaign, in 2016 over a quarter of all Fortune 500 companies clearly identified the medical expenses of transgender health and care as part of their benefits packages.[81] The gay and transgender rights group began analyzing corporate benefits for transgender employees in 2002. At that time, no health insurance plans at these companies were transgender-inclusive, but the 2015 statistics are a nineteen percent improvement over the prior year, so the trend is clearly in the right direction. In HRC's 2016 Corporate Equality Index, Chevron, Apple, and AT&T received 100-point ratings grading business's commitment to equality for LGBT employees.

EMC Corporation also received a CEI score of 100, both in 2016 and in 2015. Ranked 128 in *Fortune's* Top 1000, this data storage company with 60,000 employees based in Hopkins, Massachusetts has an inspiring success story about a transgender employee, Koset Surakomol, who decided to have a sex change operation. While this would hardly have been the case five or ten years ago, her employer took this essential decision in stride and immediately had her co-workers of a dozen years address her as a woman, no longer a man.

In addition, EMC Corp. participated in the expense of her surgeries for facial contouring, breast augmentation, and sex reassignment, in addition to hormone therapy. In fact, as *Diversity Woman* reports, EMC has offered its transgender employees who experience gender dysphoria these health benefits since 2007.

Surakomol is an information technology engineer, and she told *Diversity Woman,* "I got no bad reactions, no cold shoulders. All I heard was, 'This is wonderful.'" [82]

The U.S. Military now has policy for allowing transgender individuals to serve openly, and includes an adaptation of its health and HR provisions to address this significant change. But while the transgender community continues to gain more civil and legal protections in courts and communities across the country, they are also still experiencing setbacks and challenges to their acceptance and inclusion. Where they do, progressive *Fortune* 500 companies with deep-seated commitments to Diversity & Inclusion are stepping up as advocates and allies.

Starbucks, for example, (which has also offered transgender reassignment surgery as part of its employee health benefits package since 2013 and strives for "unconditional acceptance" of its trans employees), has taken a leadership role in fighting equality for members of the LGBTQ community, particularly in speaking out against North Carolina's discriminatory law HB2. Not only did the Starbucks CEO Howard Schultz join over 200 top CEOs in sending a letter to that state's governor and General Assembly in opposition to the bill, but Starbucks EVP Lucy Helm has reached out to all their employees to explain why these strong measures were essential.

"Consistent with our Mission and Values, and our long-standing policies and principles, Starbucks opposes any legislation or other similar policy initiatives at the municipal, state or national level that would have a discriminatory impact," Lucy Helm shared.[83]

EMC's Global Chief Diversity Officer director of benefits Delia Vetter share Starbucks's commitment to making their workplace welcoming and progressive.

As Ms. Vetter says, "Everyone has a right to be naturally happy."[84]

CHAPTER 4

THE FOUNDATION/
STRATEGIC DIRECTION

THIS CHAPTER IS DEDICATED to providing you with a framework that your company or association can use in order to develop and expand your business's diversity in ways that will also improve profits and productivity. I will lay out my strategic approach to embedding diversity and inclusion in your workforce, your workplace, your suppliers and partners, and your marketplace, and then go on to show you how to increase revenues and other key objectives through a systematic plan for diversity and inclusion.

I believe that this framework will help you to develop your own plan of attack for diversity and inclusion based on proven success for achieving business goals and objectives. Getting people motivated around D&I requires clear goals and objectives, a clear understanding of how diversity helps improve business results, as well as recognition and compensation for success. This framework will help you to align managers and affiliates with your diversity vision, and offer you strategies for incentivizing partners and stakeholders so they co-operate with your D&I philosophy through influence and persuasion when enforcement is neither possible nor appropriate.

I call this framework the Big Six. It is a pathway that is easy to adapt to your particular business, organization, corporation, or association. It is also comprehensive. And it works! While, for most organizations surveyed in late 2015 by *Talent Management* magazine, diversity and inclusion strategy is "mostly targeted toward employees" and, for 70% of those, focused on entry-level employees,[85] this Big 6 approach, which includes your customers, clients, suppliers and external partners in addition to "human assets," will show you how to maximize D&I to serve your full complement of business goals and objectives.

Let me introduce you to these six components of any successful diversity and inclusion strategic direction. Then, let's look at how it applies to you.

#1 Human Assets

As the **New Normal** demonstrates, you want diversity in every room at your company or organization. You want a full spectrum of diverse voices at the tables making decisions on products, marketing, distribution, acquisition, corporate responsibility, and HR.

This may sound obvious, but it takes both commitment and energy to achieve this essential direction. As the Deloitte report states, it's not just about sprinkling the staff with a few women and people of color. It requires, first, a commitment to making your company reflect the demographics of America at all levels of your undertaking. That includes staff from the support positions through middle management and up to those residing in the C-Suites. It includes your manufacturers and suppliers as well as your buyers and stakeholders. It also includes your corporate governance and all of the committees related to your boards and/or trustees.

Commitment to this first prong of the Big Six, **Diverse Human Assets,** particularly as it pertains to institutional governance, is guaranteed to pay off. A study done by the *Financial Review* "examines the relationship between board diversity and firm value for *Fortune* 1000 firms. Board diversity is defined as the percentage of women, African Americans, Asians, and Hispanics on the board of directors. This research is important because it presents the first empirical evidence examining whether board diversity is associated with improved financial value. After controlling for size, industry, and other corporate governance measures, (it) finds significant positive relationships between the fraction of women or minorities on the board and firm value. (It) also finds that the proportion of women and minorities on boards increases with firm size and board size, but decreases as the number of insiders increases."[86]

Automatic Data Processing is a top DiversityInc company for five years based on their comprehensive diversity initiative, led by their CEO and President Carlos Rodriguez, and focused on both a supplier-diversity program and its talent-development efforts. As Rita Mitjans, Chief Diversity & Corporate Social Responsibility Officer states it so succinctly, "At ADP, the business case for diversity and Inclusion is inextricably tied to our core business—helping clients unlock their human potential. Valuing diverse perspectives promotes innovation and employee engagement—two key drivers of corporate performance. In today's competitive marketplace, companies that excel at sustaining a diverse and inclusive workforce win."[87]

Once you have a **stated objective** of your commitment to diverse Human Assets, you then need to **establish a set of goals** as they pertain specifically to the various levels found throughout your corporation. This does not just pertain to diverse *employment and representation,* although, of course, you start there. It also involves creating goals for various key executives or departments that are connected to your company's diversity of human assets; oftentimes this involves structured incentives, compensation, and measurements.

I will discuss scorecards in the next chapter, but let me give you some examples.

Look at your leadership and key business units. Identify a goal for diverse human assets within each one. Your board of directors and principal managers should link performance compensation to various benchmarks and goals that are established and related to diversity and inclusion. Strengthen the diversity on each one of your committees, boards, and task forces, then have them each make Diversity and Inclusion a strategic focus area for the work that they do.

Do you have branches, divisions, departments, program areas, volunteer membership, or community managers?

Make diversity and inclusion a stated Strategic Focus Area for each of these business units, as well. Have top management create specific goals for inclusion or representation or for market development within various stated demographics as an annual company-wide goal. That sort of annualized statement of goals will be more easily translated into metrics than just a sweeping D&I philosophy—although you do need *both*!

Once you have goals for diversifying your human assets, you also need to **identify concrete ways to attain those goals.** It may just be a dozen single sentences, each one directed at a level of leadership, management, or governance. It may be a directive that one aspect of your company—say, the Board for one of your program areas—commits to, by establishing its own annual goal for greater diversity among some aspect of its management or committees. Perhaps you include in your recommendations for attainment strategy a specific suggestion that targets middle-management diversity and recruitment, rather than solely within emerging or entry level positions, in order to build a stronger pipeline of high-level diverse voices and viewpoints in critical strategic business units.

Sometimes, you have the opportunity to create financial incentives tied to D&I goals or can provide financial assistance that goes directly to support your targets, as a way to develop diverse talent within your organization. You might want to establish scholarships, grants, or stipends in order to increase access to your programs for diverse participants. Or perhaps it is possible to sponsor professional development designated specifically for diverse middle managers and include this as a budget line item annually.

You may have the ability to link executive compensation or performance bonuses to a manager's success in tangibly meeting corporate or divisional diversity goals. DiversityBusiness.com's 2012 Champions of Diversity winner Don Lowery (Senior Vice-President, Corporate Reputation and Public Affairs, Nielsen) encourages corporations to tie performance evaluation of senior managers—including bonus or other compensation—to meeting diversity targets. These targets will be developed after you collect and share data on your company's current diversity picture and employee views on diversity.[88]

I'll talk more about measuring your workforce and workplace diversity in Chapter 5, but you will find it helpful to survey your employees to get their views on what role D&I should play in the workforce and their perceptions on the effectiveness (or lack thereof) of existing diversity programs, as part of your process for developing ways to diversify your specific company.

One way of meeting your Human Assets diversity objectives may be to establish a dedicated diversity department, employee resource group (ERG), inclusion council, or affinity group or groups. ERGs have become a highly useful corporate tool for talent development, identification, and diversity staff management; they have traditionally been based on race, gender, or ethnicity, but they also succeed when organized around shared passions or disability issues. ERGs may also help to mitigate "employee isolation in an increasingly virtual, global, chaotic work environment" that may be having "real economic consequences" for corporations and employers.[89]

Many corporations and associations have found new ways to establish and work with ERGs strategically for a number of reasons. When properly organized and managed, these groups can support a company's specific business objectives (including and beyond diversity) in myriad ways; they also assist management in the professional development of employee leaders, thereby generating a diverse talent pipeline; and they provide insight into and access to a corporation's community and marketplace.

For example, while AT&T has been ranked by DiversityInc among its Top 50 Companies for Diversity each of the past sixteen years (in 2016, at number four), Senior Vice President-Human Resources & Chief Diversity Officer at AT&T Cynt Marshall says that the company's steadfast commitment builds on a decades-long emphasis on diversity and inclusion that perhaps began back in 1968, when AT&T launched its industry-leading supplier diversity program, but the company has also been a notable pioneer in the development and leverage of ERGS. Its LGBT ERG, LEAGUE at AT&T, was the first in the nation in 1987, and its women and African American groups—Women of AT&T and Community NETwork—are each more than forty years old.

"Employee participation in the company's ERGs and employee networks has exploded recently, with total membership exceeding 127,000, and they played a key role in integrating AT&T and DIRECTV following last year's merger. So it's no surprise that DiversityInc named the company No. 1 on its ERGs specialty list, a key factor in its No. 4 ranking overall."[90]

As Marshall goes on to say, "When employees know they matter as individuals, anything's possible. It's reassuring beyond words to know that virtually all of our employees know they matter."

ERGs can often be useful in both product development and marketing and can be very informative and instrumental in helping companies realize their goals of successful and comprehensive inclusion, as their human assets become more diverse.[91]

In a recent MIT Sloan Management review of ERGs at major companies like GE, Shell Oil, IKEA and IBM, working across various industries, a set of best practices for ERGs was identified, both for the management of human assets as well as for the realization of other key business objectives. The study found that tangible results for organizations with ERGs came about most often when there was an "alignment with strategy, internal consistency, cultural embeddedness, management involvement, balance of global and local needs, and employer branding through differentiation" in the establishment and activities of corporate ERGs.[92]

How does that work, in practice? Kraft Foods has a comprehensive approach to their ERGs that has demonstrated considerable effectiveness. The company holds employee-resource groups directly accountable for organizational initiatives. So, for instance, when Kraft established a D&I goal around the professional advancement of people of color, they turned to their African-American,

Latino, and Asian-American councils in order to work on development issues jointly with senior and HR executives.

In order to ensure that their ERGs are aligned to their diversity strategy, Kraft's diversity executives meet with them four to six times a year in order to follow up on the strategies and keep each ERG committed. Their primary focus is assistance with recruitment, employee development support, and community engagement, both inside and outside the corporation (see more on that in point 5, below). Kraft also established an Employee Council Leadership Academy which brought together the national ERG leaders for facilitated meetings and team meetings that support their people, process, and results. This made Kraft's ERG leaders even more aligned to the company's diversity strategies and focused on what they each can do in order to support those strategies.

Kraft also assigns ERGs joint initiatives and, as part of their diversity goal-setting, defines two to three areas each year for these assignments. One of them was a program called Jump Start, which navigated the unwritten rules of the Kraft Foods organization. The goal was to help new hires to understand how the place really works, and what might get them in trouble or hold them back from fitting in. A second one was a peer-coaching project, and a third focuses on minority mentoring.

Mentoring is significant as a strategy for improving the success of your inclusion goals because, according to a Greatheart Labs survey done of 700 managers at eight major companies like Pepsi Co. and Bank of America, although respect seemed consistent across cultural or racial differences, white male managers had failures in communicating.

"You don't provide the feedback you would give to the people who look like you," study author Chuck Shelton told Today.com. "Ultimately, you're discriminating because you're not allowing that person to improve and get ahead."[93]

The ERGs were engaged to review all of the mentoring programs at Kraft, and identify what was missing, so that the company could expand and improve their success at Diversity and Inclusion.

Leading multiline insurer Zurich American Insurance has several employee resource groups, notably PrideZ, "which is a growing group of both LGBT individual and allies ... committed to supporting awareness, sensitivity and inclusion of fhe LGBT workforce across Zurich," according to Zurich North America HR head Brian Little. He says that the "primary reason for his company's steadfast support of the lesbian, gay, bisexual and transgender community boils down to two simple words—'people vision.'" Since "people vision" is a core aspect of Zurich's corporate strategy, Little works to incorporate "Zurich's support and commitment to the LGBT community ... wherever possible, including in supplier diversity, outreach, workforce and human resources."[94]

Sodexo continues to improve its best-in-class IMPACT mentoring program, led by SVP and Global Chief Diversity Officer Dr. Rohini Anand. These talent-development efforts "boldster the diversity of its talent pipeline in all its business units."[95]

The 2016 top company for mentoring according to *DiversityInc* is Ernst & Young, whose partners, principals, executive directors and directors are actively engaged in leading EY's diversity and inclusion efforts as mentors, sponsors and professional network executive sponsors.

COMPANY CASE STUDY
Approach to Diversity: Walgreens, #ImInToHire

As detailed in Chapter 1, people with disabilities are a large and significant demographic whose employment and inclusion rates are far below those of the rest of the population. While 65% of those abled were reported as employed full time and 18% were employed part time in 2015 by the U.S. Bureau of Labor Statistics, only 17.5% of the persons with a disability were employed full time, 32% part time.[96]

There are some important success stories in how corporations are adapting their hiring procedures and on-site training programs to attract and integrate a broader spectrum of employee with disabilities. Walgreens, the retail pharmacy and second-largest chain in the United States, made a D&I commitment linked to their new distribution center in Anderson, S.C. that has led the way in approaching this aspect of diversity.

In this instance, the company has eight hundred new employee positions and set a benchmark to hire thirty-percent of those new employees with workers on a spectrum of developmental and intellectual disabilities. As the jobs and employment site Monster reports in *The Huffington Post*, Walgreens adapted their on-site training programs and worked with local hiring agencies to attract and onboard people with disabilities.[97] The greater aspect of this success story is that not only was Walgreens able to meet their target inclusion numbers, they exceeded them. In addition, that distribution center has come to operate twenty percent more efficiently than any of the company's others; Walgreens cites "increased productivity, lower turnover, and a highly motivated workforce.[98]

Other companies are adopting disabled worker inclusivity. The I'm In to Hire campaign launched by Best Buddies International (*#ImInToHire*) promotes the business benefits of hiring people with intellectual and developmental disabilities (IDD) and motivates employers to create a more inclusive workplace. In their most recent report, authored with the research firm the Institute for Corporate Productivity, 73% of the companies surveyed reported positive experiences employing individuals with IDD, and more than three-quarters rated their IDD employees good or very good.[99]

As Best Buddies founder Anthony Shriver said as he and billionaire industrialist Carlos Slim inaugurated the I'm in the Hire challenge to companies worldwide, "People with IDD are incredibly talented, loyal, hard-working and driven individuals who have the ability to contribute to the workplace but unfortunately they are disproportionately unemployed in our nation and beyond. "The impact individuals with IDD have made on our society is beyond exceptional and the work place should be no different."[100]

Business results are proving him truly correct!

#2 Image

Your corporate image is that mental picture that springs to mind when someone mentions your company name. It is a fluid public perception, comprised of ever-changing impressions that are based on your company's performance, coverage in the media, and what is being said about it. Sometimes—more often than not, these days, at least in part—your image is also an actual physical image: an ad, an optic at a convention or public presentation, a logo or graphic.

Your image can change overnight, from positive to negative to neutral and back again. That said, it is also something that you can influence and direct. Often it is also a major part of what sells your company or its products. *Image* is the second of the Big Six components of your Diversity and Inclusions strategy.

What do people see when they "see" your company, your product, your marketing materials, your service offerings? What can you do to display images that encourage a diverse audience to support what it is that you are selling, making, or doing? How can you bring the pictures, the key art, the photographs, the optics, and your company's photo opportunities, in line with your diversity sensitivity? How can your diversity and inclusion strategy help you to generate a smart image for your company?

For example, the USTA has made a commitment to support and encourage the participation of more Latino children in the sport of tennis. It is wonderful exercise, builds positive values, and is accessible for emerging players even in urban and low-income environments. But the USTA's ads and outreach would not have been successful merely by showing more Latino kids playing the game and participating in the association's activities.

Diversity research and deeper thinking about this demographic taught the Association that it needed to speak to the family orientation of Hispanic families. They connect with activities and organizations that involve and support the family. They want to associate with companies and institutions that share their family values. So the company needed to include and embrace all family members in our images of tennis, in order to inspire Latino community members to join, learn, and continue with this wonderful game.

Establish a set of goals for your various executives, departments, and divisions in order to improve both your company's internal and external image among diverse communities. Up in Chapter 3, you analyzed your workforce, stakeholders, audience, and markets, and you identified the **target audience** for your D&I effort. Be sure that your goals emphasize an improvement of your image with these target audience members.

You will now need to develop some **ways to attain your goals** of improving your corporate image, in order to strengthen the appeal of your company and its products for diverse audiences. Your D&I team should strategize with your communications department in order to map out the initial public relations needs of your business. Perhaps you need to design a set of culturally appropriate communications directed at your target audiences in order to generate awareness of your products, services, or corporation, in general.

A second step is to publicize your success at diversity and inclusion. Look at ways that you can spotlight your diverse staff, commend diverse volunteer leaders, promote the diversity statistics of your programs or sales, and produce then publicize events for and with your diverse workforce, stakeholders, and community members.

Your marketing executives are key partners in your implementation of diversity and inclusion priorities for your corporate image. As illuminated by the example in my introduction about the Sunset Boulevard billboard conundrum, marketing materials need to be developed with appropriate translations, multi-cultural images, and a feeling of inclusion that speaks directly to the wide complement of demographics that comprise your target audience.

Your online and social media presence has become a major component of your corporate image. Along with your marketing and D&I team, you also need to consider what language or translations are available for your digital assets, in order to expand or improve your image with various demographic groups.

Look at every page of your website and each image that accompanies an Instagram, Facebook, Snapchat, LinkedIn, Tumblr, Pinterest, YouTube, or Twitter (including video) post. Are they as diverse in age and sex, race and ethnicity and social orientation as you and your company are? How do the images on your website reflect not only ethnic and racial diversity, but also differences of ability, or non-tradition LGBT relationships and family constellations?

Which of your marketing or program materials should be in Spanish? How can your marketing department support diversity by allocating outreach and resources to community-based venues or events, ones that will improve your image or be seen in places not yet aware of your great product or services? Frito-Lay, for example, developed a separate line of tortilla chips called Tanqueros and targeted it for the cost-conscious Latino consumer in order to expand their image beyond the top-dollar snack food spectrum. They distributed Tanqueros through bodegas, dollar stores, and other discount outlets as part of a marketing and distribution shift designed to reach out to the multi-cultural consumer.[101]

What regional or national events or celebrations could expand or boost your image within select communities? I cover some of these considerations in my discussion of community engagement, below, but think about these decisions in terms of your brand image, too, and how they can forge or improve an image that reflects and inspires corporate diversity and inclusion.

Can you celebrate your commitment to diversity and advancements in inclusion with an image? Here is an example from Microsoft:

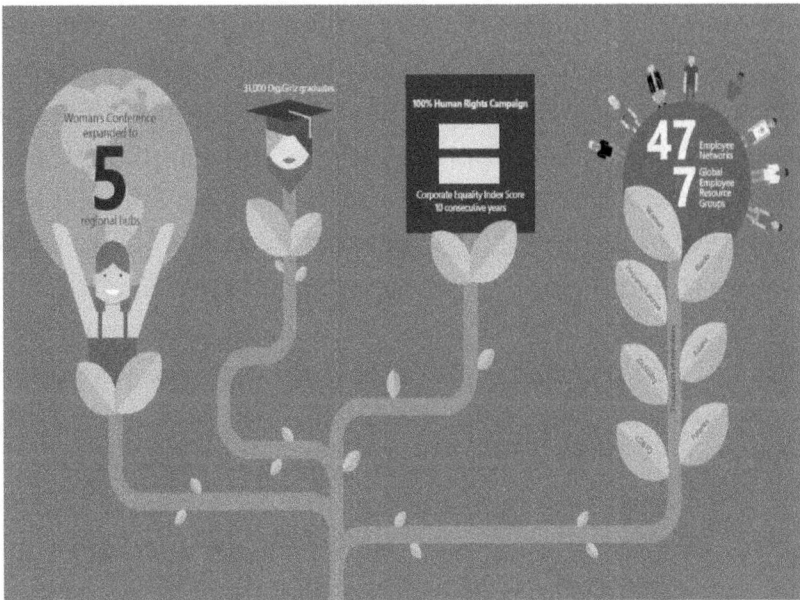

The Business of Inclusion, www.Microsoft.com © 2016

#3 Supplier Diversity

How you select your suppliers or procure your services will be a critical element of your D&I strategic direction. Setting and achieving goals to have more effective supplier-diversity efforts will both strengthen your appeal to diverse audiences **and** directly impact your bottom line through new avenues and opportunities for your business, product, or service. Companies of all sizes are developing supplier diversity programs, and many institutions, grantmakers, and RFPs both require and measure the status of this management initiative within your organization.

You would think that this would be an easy area to demonstrate swift improvement in your D&I strategy. Companies spend a lot of money, buy supplies, procure product, or do many RFPs and award contracts for goods and services. You need to make supplier diversity an actual committed part of your 6-phase plan of attack, however, because tradition and inertia work against you. The single most significant reason given for why more minority- and women-owned businesses are not used as suppliers is **because of pre-existing relationships** with or track records from male- or Caucasian-owned firms. If a firm has *been* a supplier or has a *record* for doing the work, plus they *bid it competitively* and no problems have been reported with their service, it is often hard to move business, contracts, or commitments over to a new or different firm.

But it is worth doing for many reasons, not least of which is that new, diverse supplier relationships will extend your outreach and market research. It is also worthwhile to enlist the commitment of the rest of your company to explore these new contracts and relationships, in order to improve your engagement with diverse suppliers.

Any time that demographics shift, executives have found that suppliers from traditionally underrepresented groups are one of the very best sources for new ways to reach populations whose buying power is on the rise. According to the Selig Center for Economic Growth, the combined purchasing power of Hispanic and Asian consumers was $2 trillion in 2015 and will grow to $2.8 trillion by 2020. Buying power of African-Americans was an additional $1.2 trillion and heading to $1.4 trillion by 2020.

"The Asian and Hispanic markets will really drive the U.S. consumer market," said Jeff Humphreys, director of the Selig Center for Economic Growth. "Those two groups will account for a disproportionate amount of growth. ... The

Asian Indian subgroup is actually smaller in population than the Chinese subgroup, but their per capita buying power is just off the charts," he added.[102]

One of the first steps for your company is to recognize the value of relationships with MWBEs. It is highly likely that they have their fingers on the pulse of a multicultural consumer base.

Where you can create or expand a diversely-managed division or can support a minority- or woman-owned business enterprise (MBEs and WBEs), you will see a ripple effect. When companies obtain goods and services from traditionally underrepresented groups, both parties thrive and the local economy gets a boost. Everyone wins.

The numbers don't lie. By changing your diversity supplier relationships, you stand to benefit from a $100+ billion market for goods and services. Business-to-business companies often need to meet supplier diversity requirements of either their government contracts or their customers. Business-to-consumer organizations find direct market value in their supplier diversity initiatives, because they offer greater market penetration, improve your firm's image and reputation, plus bring myriad social and economic benefits directly back to your company.[103]

So, as the key demographic groups that constitute of the **New Normal** gain traction and visibility, more corporations are embracing the use of Black-, Latino-, Asian- and women-owned suppliers as a business strategy. Some companies have also expanded their supply base to include companies owned by veterans, LGBT managers, and people with disabilities. Part of the ripple effect is that demand like yours is expanding the number of MBWEs to choose from.

Ralph G. Moore of RGMA, recognized as one of the world's foremost experts in the area of supplier diversity, urges taking your supplier diversity "to the next level," starting with quantifying the value proposition it offers you and your company, including what it "costs" and what it "pays" to diversify your spending goals and supplier development requirements. You can even incorporate supplier diversity goals into your sales contracts and *your* supplier's contracts, requiring proof of compliance while possibly creating "supplier of the year" incentives.[104]

I think that, once you begin to implement a Supplier Diversity strategy through my recommendations, below, you will agree with Ramona Blake, Global Diversity and Inclusion Practitioner at United Technologies Corporation in Hartford. "Supplier diversity is just good business," she says. These suppliers have brought her unique insights and an entrepreneurial energy that has helped her company and many others retain a competitive advantage. In addition, while working as diversity manager for PSEG, Blake observed that contracting with MBEs and WBEs had a "multiplier effect" that increased spending and consumption and promoted job creation on a local level, as well.

Hyatt, another industry leader, has developed an extensive supplier diversity program, according to their VP Global Diversity and Inclusion Tyronne Stoudemire. As they state clearly about their program on their website, "In our efforts to increase our overall purchasing with minority and women-owned businesses, we established benchmarks/goals for our managed properties. To help us reach our goals, we contracted with CVM Solutions, a company that provides supplier relationship management tools to manage the location, registration, and qualification of suppliers."

And, of course, this program is in support of the company's overall diversity mission. "At Hyatt, we are building and sustaining a culture where everyone is embraced and valued for who they are so they can be their best," Stoudemire states. "This enables Hyatt to provide authentic hospitality that cares and engages every guest and every colleague worldwide."

The agricultural producer Cargill has more than 2,500 suppliers, including multinational corporations and farms in developing countries. According to Cargill's director of supplier diversity, John Taylor, a diverse supply chain is a chance to engage local markets and to participate in community activities. "We're a global company," he says. "We would like our supplier base to reflect that." He, too, notes that working with diverse vendors has also benefitted Cargill's customers, by creating additional jobs within the communities where they live and work.[105] "The diversity of our supply chain is one of the many ways we offer distinctive value to our customers—by fostering economic growth in the communities they serve."

The beginning of your approach to improving supplier diversity begins with thinking through those aspects of your business that service local communities. Then do an across-the-board analysis of how your firm or organization spends money. Where can you allocate funds or increase the percentage of your spending with certified diverse vendors and suppliers? With your senior staff, look at each division or business unit, and **establish goals** for increasing these percentages or overall amounts in your next year.

Many companies, organizations, and associations have Supplier Diversity programs or initiatives. Perhaps you need to establish one or strengthen them in each of your divisions, chapters, regions, or business units. Recent analysis of data on *Fortune 100* and *Global 1000* companies offer insight into corporate spending efforts and best practices that should inspire you, and provide guidance on implementing this component of your D&I strategy.

Supplier diversity contributes directly to your competitive advantage. It offers you new ways to partner with key minority stakeholders. And it gives you insight into the needs and interests of minority markets. Cargill's diversity supplier director acknowledges these benefits from partnering with a multicultural supply base. "MWBEs have very good insight with regard to the products and services that they are offering and can bring that market intelligence to Cargill," says Taylor. Looking to capitalize on this market intelligence, the company has increased its supplier-diversity spend by nine percent each year for the past four. Wells Fargo has had a goal of spending $1 billion annually with diverse-owned business enterprises since 2013.[106]

Despite a small, short downturn in corporate spending with diverse suppliers during the 2008-2009 economic slow-down, all data since 2010 shows a return to steady upward trends in the billions of dollars spent annually with minority firms. Those companies with "world-class procurement functions" spend 33% more each year on diverse suppliers than typical companies which, according to the *Graziadio Business Review,* generates "133% greater returns in the cost of procurement ... driving an additional $3.6 million to their company's bottom line."[107]

You can improve your supplier diversity by aligning your program objectives with decisions about the number of diverse suppliers with whom they work. Remember: you're thinking about ways to connect both with local communities and with a variety of diverse demographics through your allocation of supplier dollars. The Hackett study found that "while the objectives of business-to-business companies might be best served by focusing on a few larger contracts to satisfy government regulations, business-to-consumer companies seeking to drive market awareness and penetration should consider focusing their supplier diversity efforts on developing a larger group of suppliers and smaller individual contracts.[108]

Consider increasing the percentage of your company's suppliers that your diversity suppliers represent. Think in terms of goals and metrics. Remember that each one of your programs has a supplier budget, as do various divisions or departments. You can work on establishing diversity supplier goals within each way.

Health Care Service Corporation (HCSC/Blue Cross Blue Shield of Illinois) looks at the diversely-owned businesses that have become their suppliers as well as local ambassadors of their company's values. "We're committed to our diverse community," says Malinda Burden, HCSC's senior director, so she commits her company to partnerships with MWBE "because it adds value to what we do, as well as promotes prosperity in the communities we serve."

Wells Fargo has a similar appreciation for its supplier-diversity program, which expanded in 2009 to include veteran-, disabled veteran- and LGBT-owned businesses. According to their senior vice president and Head of Corporate Supplier Diversity Regina Edwards, this change in suppliers has increased profits and reduced bid response time, plus it inspires and engages Wells Fargo's employees, another boost to Human Assets!

"When our suppliers have different experiences, perspectives, cultures and backgrounds," she says, "we receive the most innovative, creative and cost-effective products and services available."[109]

So, **how do you realize your supplier diversity** goals? Metrics are a great tool here. You can establish annual goals for achieving greater supplier diversity within each department, division, or business unit. Encourage each of them to set their own annual goals, as well, then work with staff and leadership to achieve these goals. They may need parameters for outreach, bid evaluation, or new relationships within the supplier community when asked to stretch beyond traditional suppliers and firms. Consider recommending that they utilize the resources provided by **the National Minority Supplier Development Council** (www.NMSDC.org), as a tool for connecting their needs with minority-owned businesses.

Most firms that have seen marked success in their supplier-diversity efforts have broadened the number and the types of firms that provide them with goods and services.

It does not just apply to your raw materials: consider who provides your firm with legal and finance services, or the floors and construction materials of your offices and remodeling; who manages your information systems; who provides employee benefits packages, and so on. Take an across-the-board look at where your company spends money, and see how it can be used to support your D&I strategy.

Major corporations like AT&T and/or Allstate, which spend millions and billions on their supplier-diversity programs and have developed their best practices over many years, identify some activities and initiatives that have contributed to their success. Could these help you improve on your action plan?

These best practices include mentoring programs for new multi-cultural suppliers who can be trained to meet a business' needs, or mentored to become competent in particular areas of concern to a contractor.[110] They also recognize that financial and education support alone won't expand the reach of these suppliers unless they have access to the company decision-makers.

In recognizing the top 2016 companies for supplier diversity, topped by AT&T, Dell, Accenture, Hilton, and Comcast NBCUniversal, *DiversityInc* underscores the following as strategies for success in achieving "higher percentages of both Tier I (direct contractor) and Tier II (subcontractor) procurement with vendors owned by women, Blacks, Latinos, Asians, American Indians, LGBT individuals, people with disabilities and veterans with disabilities:

- ❖ Integrating supplier diversity into corporate goals
- ❖ Having the CEO sign off on supplier-diversity results
- ❖ Auditing supplier-diversity numbers
- ❖ Ensuring suppliers are certified
- ❖ Linking procurement-management compensation to supplier-diversity goals"[111]

Both AT&T and Allstate conduct matchmaking events or supplier-diversity exchanges, where many minority-owned businesses are introduced to either their own various business divisions or even to competitors, as a way of offering networking and community service as well as improve the firm's own relationship with the diversity-supplier businesses.[112] PSEG hosts annual supplier-diversity fairs at no charge, as well. As a direct result of these procurement events, that company has awarded more than thirty-seven contracts to new MBEs and WBEs.[113]

AT&T established a "Women of Color Business Growth Initiative." In 2010, they graduated seven minority-women-owned businesses after training them in ways to access capital, develop sustainability plans, and use business technology. Each one has gone on to become a supplier to this and other participating corporations.[114] AT&T was also named one of the Best 10 Corporations for Veteran-Owned Businesses by Vetrepreneur Magazine, and "Operation Hand Salute," an AT&T program for disabled-veteran business enterprises, graduated five DVBEs who now have the tools and expertise needed to win large corporate contracts.

Wells Fargo's Leaders of Change program takes a holistic approach to supplier engagement and development. It sponsors MWBE suppliers to attend leadership training at Dartmouth's Tuck School of Business and Northwestern University's Kellogg School of Management. It partners with industry advocacy organizations to provide classroom training to suppliers. It also offers one-on-one coaching and mentoring opportunities for MWBEs with expert consultants in business-strategy planning and operational improvement. And it develops young and emerging entrepreneurs through collaborations with various universities and organizations. Wells Fargo looks on its supplier diversity initiative as an investment on many levels destined to pay off handsomely.[115]

Strengthening diverse businesses contributes to the overall economic success of the communities where you, your customers, and your staff live and work. Staples' Supplier Diversity Program has selected the following diverse businesses for intense focus in their supply chain: Small Disadvantaged Businesses (SDB), Minority-Owned Business Enterprise (MBE), Women-Owned Business Enterprise (WBE), Disabled Business Enterprise (DIS), Veteran-Owned Businesses (VBE) and HUBZone Businesses.[116]

Arkansas-based national big-box chain Walmart has been vocal and visible about encouraging diverse companies to register with the company as a diverse supplier. More than 3,000 diverse companies have completed the first step in reaching up to 140 million customers each week. Michael A. Byron, Senior Director of Supplier Diversity, "firmly believes that thinking like a merchant is the strongest differentiator of the program.

"'I see myself as an advocate for our customers and suppliers,' he said. 'As a Walmart associate, I am also a merchant, striving to meet the needs of our customers by fostering a truly inclusive supply chain. We've very thoughtfully and intentionally partnered with diverse suppliers. Our team spends a significant amount of time understanding the business model of our diverse suppliers and offering suggestions on how, together, we can grow our collective businesses and provide solutions for our customers.'

"Growth and participation in the program are measured annually and the results of the 2014 Supplier Diversity Impact Study share a compelling story of Walmart's diverse suppliers and the impact on their employees and communities. For instance, diverse suppliers who responded to the study indicated they are small-to-large, family-owned businesses with 20 percent of their annual revenues coming from Walmart sales. In addition, respondents typically employ an ethnically diverse group of individuals and heavily patronize minority-owned businesses."[117]

Walmart also holds an annual Supplier Summit, where buyers and suppliers find a supportive environment to share expertise and insights while company executives like Byron can gather intel to fine tune their approach to suppliers.

Another key driver of the success of Walmart's supplier diversity program is that "diversity and inclusion initiatives are supported at the highest level of the organization ... The support received from the CEO, senior leaders and associates has empowered Supplier Diversity to deliver on its mission "to embed our supplier diversity program into the company's overall business objectives" and to articulate the value of inclusion in all business outcomes."[118]

The final benefit of expanding your supplier diversity is the way in which it invites entrée and access to a wide variety of communities. Each supplier is connected to markets and consumers, each has unique intelligence into the needs and habits of a variety of demographic groups, so each one is a resource as much as a statistic. Think of your women- and minority-owned business suppliers as real allies in the diverse and constantly evolving markets we have been discussing. You, too, can use them as regional ambassadors and proof that your company is the sustainable growth of diverse communities a stated and significant priority.

Your commitment to diverse suppliers also becomes part of your corporate image and messaging. Use your supplier diversity to commit to your target communities.

Expand it, and then talk about it. You'll see what I mean!

COMPANY CASE STUDY

Approach to Diversity: Nationwide

Nationwide, the insurance and financial services organization, has been recognized by *Black Enterprise* and *Latina Style* magazines for their diversity and inclusion and by Human Rights Campaign and *Forbes* as a great place to work for minority employees. Under the leadership of CEO Stephen Rasmussen, "We embrace differences because it helps to make our company great."

Along with Mr. Rasmussen, Nationwide's diversity head, EVP and CAO Gayle King, has led efforts at corporate diversity through their in-depth supplier diversity program designed to "foster the promotion, growth and development of minority, women, lesbian, gay and veteran-owned enterprises." The company credits the program with playing an important role in developing Nationwide's diverse suppliers and helping the company determine whether various of their products or services would fit within Nationwide's corporate strategies.

Andrew D. Walker, President of Nationwide Bank (a subsidiary of Nationwide Insurance, where he was chief procurement officer) says, "The diversity of our associates—and by extension our external suppliers—is an absolute strength. The more points we engage, the more we can accomplish together."

Walker led Nationwide's sourcing and procurement, including the supplier diversity organization, before his promotion to the Bank, and won awards for what *Affinity Inc*

Magazine calls his "people-first" strategy. "As long as the topic of diversity and inclusion has been around, we can never take for granted the fact that it's one of those things that when it's encouraged from your most senior leaders, it becomes entrenched in the organization fairly easily," Walker says. "We have the strong belief that when our leaders embrace and sponsor initiatives, the rest of the organization gets on board, and we see that repeatedly." [119]

Nationwide's Office of Supplier Diversity focuses on contracting with, educating, investing in, and mentoring diverse suppliers. The company's program began as a strategic initiative in 1994 and evolved to include supplier diversity and inclusion at every level of the company. Each year, they conduct a free Supplier Development Series which is offered free to a population of diverse suppliers and led by representative LGBT, female and minority suppliers as educators and mentors.

Because the company values diversity and "understands the challenges facing minority, women, and small businesses," their Supplier Development office collaborates with their Supply Management Services to address both the bottom-line and the company's D&I benchmarks and objectives.

When *Fortune* recognized Nationwide for a second year as one of the top 100 places to work in March 2016, it was in part for the company's ongoing commitment to diversity. As regional VP and sixteen-year associate Ramon Jones said, "Nationwide has enabled and inspired me to continue to grow both personally and professionally. With a strong emphasis on diversity and inclusion, its culture aligns with my values. Performance is expected and rewarded. It is truly a great place to work."[120]

#4 Regions/Community Engagement

Your D&I action plan has looked at the tremendous human resources within your company as opportunities for great strides in diversity, as well as at the image that your company projects and the suppliers from whom you buy. You also have a great chance to directly impact your growth and success by leveraging diversity and inclusion with your customers and their communities. Your national or global D&I plan should allow for different strategies and programs so that you can specifically address the regional needs or cultural differences of the communities you serve.

Next, make a strategic commitment to improve diversity & inclusion *in every region, section, and community* in which you do business or want to do business. Your community engagement and local, regional, or sectional D&I initiatives are one of the key levers that will drive your corporate bottom line.

As I discussed in the **New Normal**, today's workforce and marketplace is a dynamic mix of different cultures, ages, races, lifestyles, genders and more. U.S. census statistics clearly prove that your consumer base and talent pools are shifting. These visible demographic differences, as well as emerging market realities, continuously create new customer and employee needs.

You may have direct control or management of your regional- or state-based corporate divisions or sales teams. On the other hand, you may need to work with local or regional providers that are more loosely connected to your corporate structure, and make sure that they become aligned with what it is that you want to accomplish in terms of your diversity and inclusion goals. In some instances, you can set goals with them, establish mandates, and enforce policies around D&I practice and metrics. In other situations, however, your relationship is different, so you need to find ways to strongly encourage, incentivize, influence and persuade your sectional or regional management.

Ultimately, as part of your Strategic Direction, you want to show your regional, sectional, or community partners how to improve their revenues and attain their objectives through leveraging diversity and inclusion. And you want to explore every opportunity for your company to engage with diverse sectors of your market, on a community level.

As Wells Fargo's Executive Vice President Michelle Lee describes it, her bank "is only as strong as the communities we serve." The financial-services company demonstrates its commitment to the Black, Latino, Asian, American Indian and LGBT communities through its deep effort to reach diverse suppliers, as well as youth and low-income people. For example, 65% percent of the executives in the top two levels of her company sit on the board of a multicultural nonprofit.

Wells Fargo also demonstrates its commitment to engagement with diverse communities through its philanthropy. For example, the company achieved its goal to lend $1 billion to Black-owned small businesses by 2008; they extended that goal to $2 billion by 2018. In 2010, the company provided $61.1 million in grants to nonprofits that were focused on community development in distressed communities, and that sought to provide local citizens with affordable housing, homeownership counseling, financial education, workforce development and job creation.[121]

Another company, J.W. Marriott, combined its community engagement with supplier diversity initiatives, and in so doing has developed a long corporate history of creating community wealth by using local minority- and women-owned business enterprises (MBEs and WBEs) to build and service its hotels, especially in urban areas.

The structure of your corporation or organization will dictate how it is that you adopt this prong of the Big Six into your D&I Action Plan. For instance, if you are part of a national corporation that has regional or sectional leaders, you can begin to build your community engagement goals in collaboration with them, helping them to develop specific ideas for leveraging diversity and inclusion in order to grow their sales and penetration.

However, if you are developing a D&I plan for an organization that has more independent regions, sections, or chapters, you may be more involved first in setting their general business or expansion goals, then persuading them to align their activities and commitments with your institutional diversity priorities in order to attain their objectives.

"To know thy own target audience" could be the mantra of today's successful marketing campaigns, and recent research has shown this to be no more true than in the swiftly expanding Latino market. The Association of Hispanic Advertising Agencies did a recent study of generational segments with the Hispanic demographic—Millennials, GenXers and Boomers—and discovered unique consumer buying patterns. AHAA learned that how each segment views the marketplace is influenced by a combination of macro-trends of their respective age-group, as well as by their lifestage priorities, and by their cultural orientation.[122] If your community-based or regional marketing and sales teams are not fluent with local markets to this degree of specificity, they will be missing out on huge swaths of opportunity. In order to use the diverse opportunities of community engagement in order to identify new business-building opportunities and improve your bottom line, you will need to develop goals and a mechanism to discern the differences in buying behavior of these and many other segments, as well as learn how they compare to their general market counterparts.[123]

Your efforts in community or regional engagement will be extremely informative. As Dr. Rohini Anand, Senior Vice President & Global Chief Diversity Officer of Sodexo says, "A richly diverse and multi-faceted workforce compels us to engage in dialogue, collaborate on new ideas, and build successful partnerships. With 428,000 employees coming from 134 nationalities working in 80 countries, Sodexo represents the diversity of today's world."[124]

University Hospitals CEO Thomas F. Zenty III puts it, "The point is, we need to look into the community to better understand who are the communities that we serve? Who best represents those individuals within those communities that we serve? And how can we engage them at every level, either as employees, as members of the board, as leadership-council members? And we want to make sure that we're engaging ***everyone*** in the communities that we serve."[125]

Your initial goal-setting in this part of your D&I action plan may involve analyzing your cities, states, and regions, identifying the target communities that comprise them, then matching either your goals or your ways to reach them with your new intelligence. Many times, you will find both a need and an opportunity within a given local community that offers you a great way for your company either to reach or expand into a new or growing market segment.

For example, Charmaine Brown is the former director of diversity and inclusion for Forest City Enterprises (FCE), a national real-estate company. During her time there, she developed community partnerships that helped Blacks and Latinos gain experience and jobs in the Cleveland area. For example, Brown led the launch of Cleveland's Real Estate Associate Program (REAP), a program that educated the city's first class of Black, Latino and Asian professionals in commercial real estate and provided networking opportunities.[126]

Brown relates her efforts back to a key lesson from her childhood. "My mom always said, 'You need to be someone [not because you are Black] but because you are Charmaine. If you do that, you will empower your race," recalls Brown.

Like other diversity executives and leaders of best practices in community engagement across the country, Brown actively participated on behalf of Forest City in several organizations for economic inclusion, including the Commission on Economic Inclusion and the Northern Ohio Minority Supplier Development Council. She also included supplier diversity in her outreach and engagement efforts by seeing to it that her organization certifies MBEs, and then provides them with networking and resources. She continues to help companies and clients meet their diversity and inclusion objectives at her new consulting company, Connexions Consulting.

Pacific Gas and Electric Company (PG&E) uses their participation in San Francisco Lunar New Year festivals as a way to provide Bay Area Chinese-American communities with information on the utility's financial assistance, energy efficiency, and their scholarship programs. PG&E tapped a Chinese senior vice president, Fong Wan, to represent the company at these events, and to activate the company's own InspirAsian Employee Resource Group (ERG) to attend and reach out to the community during the festivals.

"Lunar New Year is a special time of renewal and giving thanks, during which we sweep away the misfortunes of the past in order to welcome prosperity, good luck, and excellent health for the future," said Wan. "PG&E is honored to join Chinese-American communities in celebrating this significant occasion...and to use this opportunity to better engage our Chinese customers on various energy-saving tips through social media."[127]

Led by diversity pioneer and Global Chief Diversity Officer Patricia Harris, the McDonald's Corporation focuses its community engagement on various levels. McDonald's Founder Ray Kroc used to say, "We have an obligation to give something back to the community that gives so much to us," so exercises its commitment to being a good neighbor in thousands of local communities where McDonald's restaurants operate, particularly by leveraging their franchisees within the communities they serve to give back, both through addressing local needs for education and physical activity as well as improving the lives of children and their families through support of the Ronald McDonald House Charities.

ERGs and regional groups, like the Black McDonald's Operators Association® collaborate with the national and international management efforts to express the company's collective commitment; franchise owners within local communities help Ms. Harris and Director of Diversity & Inclusion, Global Inclusion & Community Engagement H Walker to bring awareness to the many programs and support systems that McDonald's performs in area of health, education, the arts, civil and social services.[128]

PG&E enlists their Black Employees Association, BEA ERG both to celebrate Black History Month with African American communities in Northern and Central California, but also to commemorate the history and contributions of the utility's African Americans employees, and to participate in the company's scholarship program for college-bound students in the community.

You also have an opportunity, in your corporate giving and social responsibility departments, to connect philanthropy with other community engagement programs. As you set your goals for regional or local engagement, look at ways to connect your company's charitable donations with other community involvement activities. This will maximize the impact of your giving campaign because recent trends show that "social investment" can increase impact, at a lower cost, by providing a mix of benefits of greater value to partners through more efficient means for your company.[129]

Philanthropy is an excellent leading indicator of corporate (and personal) intent.[130] Think about this, both in your analysis and in your goal-setting with national and regional executives. Both diversity and profitability are about relationships, so you want your community engagement efforts as well as your corporate giving strategy to make that connection. You will also see that a company's budget for its D&I program is directly related to how your company values connections with the community.

How are you going to go about reaching your community engagement goals? Where you have regions or local management, one step is look at their "needs," and see if some of your D&I solutions can help them achieve their identified goals and objectives. Some regions or departments may need funding that specifically supports their D&I efforts or that permits them to engage in events, sponsorships, or other opportunities for outreach to specific communities.

You may be able to design and produce "How to Reach" toolkits for various divisions, sections, or regions that want to attract specific target audiences that you have identified in your D&I strategic plan. You can do the research and messaging for them, in association with your marketing and PR departments, thereby greatly enhancing their capacity for success.

Sometimes it is helpful to design "test" or "pilot" programs on an activity, a product, or an avenue of community engagement that targets one part of your D&I goals. You could work with your division or region to try it out; department store Macy's developed a *quinceañeras* card, for example, and introduced it first in select stores based in Latino neighborhoods in order to learn how it would appeal to families shopping for their teenage girls' big celebration. Where that new micro-program or marketing direction demonstrates success in enhancing community involvement or response, it can be replicated in other regions or for additional demographics.

JPMorgan Chase states as part of its community engagement and philanthropic mandate that it "strives to be a catalyst for meaningful, positive and sustainable change in high-need neighborhoods and communities across the globe." The firm has designed what it calls a "holistic approach" to community relationships, the Pathways to Opportunity, which aim "to ensure that individuals have access to the knowledge, skills, resources, and capital they need to secure their futures and compete in the global economy." Chase's strategy is to make philanthropic investments in cities where it has major operations in order to transform low-income neighborhoods.

Community engagement can target communities or audiences, like you did with your D&I strategic plan, and then find ways to reach them through community-based initiatives. Chase, for example, engages nonprofit organizations in its key cities, along with residents, and other sources of public and private advocacy and funding, and currently focuses its investment and attention on four pillars: affordable housing, economic development, financial empowerment, and workforce readiness.[131]

#5 Strategic Partnerships

Look at the strategic partnerships that your company has or could develop as tools to build your diverse staff, markets, suppliers, and customers. Partnering with special interest organizations is an essential step in fostering relationships and bolstering recruitment efforts within different demographic segments.[132]

Companies that develop partnerships with special interest groups identify the significant role they can play in building relationships with demographic segments such as women, people of color, people with disabilities, and those in the gay, lesbian, bisexual, and transgender community. Companies that partnered with organizations focused on LGBT people have reported in very recent studies that a majority (92.3%) of them identify as having had success with increasing their corporate visibility, expanding their community outreach, and enhancing positive recruitment opportunities. 84% have equivalent good experiences with African-American groups, while 69.2 percent had positive results working with women's groups.[133]

Most businesses and non-governmental organizations (NGOs) that develop collaborations and partnerships to advance their diversity, inclusion, and social goals are engaged in 11-50 or more partnerships. They identify specific benefits that accrue from these collaborations, when undertaken correctly and effectively.

The Hershey Company uses community engagement to promote diversity and inclusion at the company. "Business resource groups (BRGs)—including the Abilities First, African American, and Veterans BRGs—facilitate the company's partnerships with diverse community groups."[134] They have found that "these partnerships strengthen the diverse voices within the company and provide a key insight into a swath of consumers."

When corporations or associations make alliances with diverse organizations through sponsorships or partnerships, companies find that they can enhance their brands, and attract new clients or customers plus develop social media or other relationships with this new base. They also improve employee retention and recruitment through building these connections with diverse partners and the issues they address, which also helps to expand corporate image or reputation within their communities. In addition, they gain unique insight into new, diverse markets that often does not come readily through other sorts of outreach or research. In fact, on a business level, based on a five-year study of sponsorship spending, companies that invested in consistent sponsorships above average levels were shown to outperform those that invested below average or not at all.[135]

If you manage an association or non-profit organization, you probably already know that sponsorships or partnerships with for-profit companies bring you not just increased funding but greater public recognition, a better image, and oftentimes access to valuable corporate resources. Businesses like professional sports franchises often sponsor local non-profits or do alliances with regional NGOs as a way to develop interest in their events and to build loyalty within critical home markets. They have found these sorts of partnerships as ideal ways to research and develop new communities of fans, or to build new support for a sport in various regions.[136]

As you and your Diversity and Inclusion department set out to analyze which strategic partnerships can improve your D&I plan and make significant contributions to your bottom line, let me give you some tips and best practices to enhancing these alliances and to ensuring that you reap the greatest rewards from any sponsorships that you make.

First, you need a clear alignment between your goals and values and those of any non-profit or company you elect to partner with. This is something to discuss right up front, before going any deeper into plans for collaboration around your diversity and inclusion efforts. For example, the US Business Leadership Network works to "build workplaces, marketplaces, and supply chains that are inclusive of people with disabilities." That's the NGOs mission. So USBLN executive director Jill Houghton ensures complimentary values with her corporate sponsors that provide 70% of her annual budget. She makes sure that her corporate partners demonstrate their own "commitment to creating equal access for all people—that commitment extends to employees, customers and suppliers," Houghton says. "It's not just the right thing to do, but it's central to their business and their culture. We're the bridge connecting companies, affiliates, allies and certified, disability-owned suppliers."[137]

Second, the value proposition for both NGO and company should be clear. You want to define it concisely before moving forward with a sponsorship or alliance. Of course, it should benefit both entities and, while the money given is a critical component, companies also need to work creatively with their non-profit partners and build a good relationship in order to realize the maximum benefit back to the corporation.

For example, Wells Fargo participates in LGBT Pride Month, but developed a specific partnership with Eliza Byard, Executive Director of GLSEN (Gay, Lesbian & Straight Education Network) in order to emphasize anti-bullying, a core inclusion value of the company's. So, while part of its sponsorship of the New York and San Francisco pride parades in June, Wells Fargo employees distributed information about GLSEN's Safe Space Campaign, and committed to continue the partnership for three years. "Wells Fargo is helping us reach more than 75,000 schools, serving 25 million students, during the three-year Safe Space Campaign," Byard says. "That's a visibility opportunity we would not have had otherwise."[138]

Comcast, one of the world's largest broadcasting, cable, and entertainment companies, sponsors "about 100 internal and external leadership development pipeline programs," which create "numerous opportunities to infuse the company with knowledgeable, engaged, creative talent." The flagship program is internal, their Executive Leadership Forum, but they also partner with Wharton in their two-year-old Women in Leadership program and many others. Their fourteen African American senior managers are a clear byproduct of inclusion and of the success of partnerships that align with their business goals.[139]

Third, be sure that you do a sponsorship agreement with any partners or non-profits, and define expectations and deliverables for both sides. This may be money and advertising/promotion and other co-branded collateral materials, but also photos with key stakeholders, eBlasts or access to digital information on members or participants.

You have corporate assets that can help your partners achieve their goals, particularly through your Diversity and Inclusion initiatives. The multi-year agreement between American Airlines, for example, and the United Negro College Fund (UNCF) ensures that the company receives a high-profile effort to promote its brand, and to engage "customers in supporting children, education, and equality."[140] The non-profit, in turn, receives critical funding for its programs, as well as a broad dissemination of information about its mission and services.

Fourth, be sure that any partnership you undertake is socialized with stakeholders both inside and outside of all organizations involved, in order to ensure their support and maximize your opportunities. For example, the Consortium for Graduate Study in Management was founded in 1966 to "reduce the under-representation of African Americans, Native American and Hispanic Americans in education and business." Its partners are over 70 major corporations including Johnson & Johnson, 3M, and General Mills. The sponsors provide over $23 million in revenue each year, which the Consortium distributes to vetted MBA candidates, providing over 8,500 MBA scholarships as of 2016. Each partner finds their image and commitment to diversity enhanced by their association with this prestigious and concrete program. The participating companies also have the chance to hire top, diverse, and well-trained talent that have been pre-selected by the Consortium's rigorous application process. So companies can "achieve their strategic goals of increasing diversity within the workplace while demonstrating a significant return on investment to stakeholders."[141] Consortium adds to the success of its mission by not only helping to educate and train to minority MBAs, but also seeing them well employed in major businesses.

Finally, you and your partners want to agree on the ways in which your contribution and outcomes can be measured and by whom. How will you evaluate the activities generated by the association or alliance? What system of metrics is appropriate—and how can you leverage those with shareholders or your community. Ideally there are steps along the way of your sponsorship, so that you can be apprised of its progress and ensure that the expectations of both parties are being met.

Some companies use the opportunity for strategic partnership as a way to incentivize employees or work more closely and effectively with ERGs and affinity groups. New York Life, for example, has a program called Volunteers for Life which encourages employees, agents, and retirees to be involved with nonprofit organizations dedicated to causes that are important to them. If an individual employee completes sixty hours of service to an organization, New York Life will provide a grant in honor of that employee. In addition, teams of five or more employees that contribute forty hours can earn a team grant. "If you're working together to do this, we want to make sure to reward it," said retired New York Life Foundation President Christine Park.[142]

There are some risks to be aware of when undertaking partnership programs as part of your D&I strategic initiative. Both you and your supported organization should be aware of the possibility that negative publicity generated by one partner can reflect badly on the other.

It is also possible that a sponsorship can be perceived as exploitation rather than as a gift or supportive effort towards a given event. If a sponsor is seen as somehow interfering with, or taking advantage of, a moment or a public spotlight, this could harm the reputation either of the event, of the sponsor, or both. When Formula 1 and its teams committed to appear at the 2013 Bahrain Grand Prix despite global controversy and public outcry after the 2012 event, 4 NGOs wrote highly publicized letters to the company and to event sponsors protesting their support of a race in a country whose government continues to commit gross human rights violations, from arbitrary arrests to torture. They asserted that Bahrain's jails contain hundreds of political prisoners, that local police use excess force with impunity, and that the country's opposition members have been stripped of their citizenship. They made clear that the 2013 Bahrain Grand Prix was an embarrassment to all those who promoted it, because it was used by the Bahrain government to broadcast a false picture of normality to the outside world, whilst also preventing entry to journalists who wanted to see the reality on the ground. In this instance, Formula 1 was being portrayed, by association, not as a sport, but as an organization that supports a repressive regime.

Finally, as I mentioned earlier, when the missions or values of partners are in misalignment, a partnership is very often unproductive or the value of the collaboration less than it could be.

More often than not, however, when well considered, partnerships are a great tool to expand your market awareness, increase your intelligence into diverse demographic groups, show off your D&I priorities, and enhance your brand in ways that will show concrete contributions to your success. Shipping giant UPS decided to withdraw its longtime support of the Boy Scouts of America in late 2012 because of its ongoing discrimination against gay scouts and leaders. Instead, UPS elected to collaborate with the Human Right Campaign on a new Workplace Project that promotes equality in the workplace by advocating for policies that prohibit discrimination against LGBT workers. The Project also seeks to attain equal benefits and diversity training for employees, and supports enlightened, inclusive marketing.

For the first time, UPS was recognized by the Gay and Lesbian Alliance Against Defamation and other prominent LGBT advocacy groups for "standing with the 80,000 Americans...who oppose the Boys Scouts' hurtful anti-gay policy." UPS was able to put its values in action, and shift its sponsorship dollars to an initiative better aligned with its own corporate Diversity and Inclusion philosophy.

There are some organizations like OBOX Solutions, run by married co-owners Tim and Thom DeWitt, designed to partner with corporate America (their clients include HP, AIG, Brink's, etc.) to complement their diversity and inclusion efforts. The first NGLCC-certified business to become a corporate partner, OBOX is a full-service staffing solution committed to "completing the circle of diversity by purchasing and doing business with other lesbian, gay, bisexual, transgender and diverse enterprises, building economic empowerment for the LGBT community."[143]

Hudson Taylor, former high school and college athlete, often observed the use of homophobic language and demeaning humor, especially in sport. He "recognized that standing up against this type of behavior as a straight ally would send a strong statement."[144] He felt it was imperative he confront the reality that sports often marginalize LGBT athletes, coaches and others through systemic homophobia and transphobia. He decided to take action as a straight ally to change athletic culture for the better. His organization, Athlete Ally, "stands in solidarity with the LGBT community" and partners across the professional and collegiate sports field to change minds, advocate for inclusion, and provide public awareness campaigns.

Today, Athlete Ally "provides educational programming and tools and resources to foster inclusive sports communities." They "mobilize Ambassadors in collegiate, professional, and Olympic sports who work to foster 'allyship' in their athletic environments. The programs include Ambassadors from over eighty colleges and over 100 professional athletes."[145]

#6 Training & Development

In order to realize your D&I strategic direction so that your company receives the maximum business benefits, it is important to encourage *all* of your employees to think about how they can promote D&I in all of their activities, from working on specific projects to the hiring of outside vendors and consultants. Oftentimes, this will involve your establishing training and professional development initiatives for managers and employees in order to orientate them to your company's goal of promoting diversity. As you can tell from the other 5 planks of this Action Plan, your company's D&I efforts should not be left only to the professionals in human resources. You need to make it part of your entire corporate, association, or organization culture.

Think about the language that you and your top executives use around diversity. I am concerned when I hear phrases like a "vision" for diversity or an "aspiration" to inclusion. Does your company's CEO have a "vision" for profitability? Does the product being developed in an engineering department have an "aspirational" diameter? Does your marketing EVP charge her sales team with an "ideal" for a sales goal? No. It's just not precise business language. D&I management is just as important a business process as any other in your company. So it should be treated that way, through company-wide efforts.

You may need to start with a goal of redesigning and delivering skill-based diversity and inclusion training company-wide. The **goal** here is as simple as that. D&I training should help people develop relationships to people who are not like them. A person's ability to build equitable relationships is directly relevant to their effectiveness in business. So this is an economic imperative.

Companies cannot afford to exclude anyone from their business operations! Not with our economy expanding to the point where our workforce was over eighty percent women and/or Black, Asian and Latino last year! "Not when household income for Black, Asian, and Latino households is rising at twice the rate of white households (and has been since 1990), where more people with ADA-defined disabilities have college degrees than people without ADA-defined disabilities, white people will be less than 50 percent of our population by 2043, gay marriage now legal in fifty states, and equal rights for all right around the corner."[146]

You want to look at ways to conduct training that supports diversity-management excellence, whether for your C-Suite executives, boards of directors, middle managers, and all department and regional leadership. You also want to frame this from a business standpoint: your company cannot be competitive for talent or succeed at maximum retention if you cannot create the right culture to attract and retain the very best people in your workforce. You need to organize training that teaches your managers what to look for in terms of problematic issues related to inclusion, and you need to help them bridge gaps in knowledge and experience between themselves and members of your target groups.

Your ability to ingrain diversity and inclusion in your company's culture starts with making D&I a corporate value. Your CEO and heads of business units need to make clear statements of these values, and then monitor and enforce them. I've shared some Diversity Statements from various top corporate websites: this is an ideal place for your company to state its own D&I mission and clarify its expectations. These pronouncements don't just spread the mission throughout your corporate culture; they also display your diversity and inclusion achievements in ways that help to attract and retain both employees and customers.

In addition to training, you may want to consider establishing a cultural audit or assessment of your corporate workforce, with measurements of change that can be critical indicators of the ways in which diversity and inclusion are embraced across the company. I'll discuss various strategies for benchmarking in the next chapter, but the inclusion of D&I values and other cultural components in your employee surveys help your company recommit itself to the formal process I have been describing for defining a mission, vision and ethics that embrace D&I.

You will be able to develop a more comprehensive culture for diversity and inclusion when you include your company's communication team in your formulation of D&I strategies and trainings. Also utilize your general counsel's input to ensure that values-related expectations are clear and cogent in employee manuals, contracts, and ERG charters. Establishing a C-level Diversity Officer, ethics, or culture officer and allocating assets to their work on a D&I plan have become best practices for ingraining diversity into a company's culture, as well.[147] While a late 2015 survey by Human Capital Media Advisory Group (the research arm *Talent Management* magazine) found a quarter of 158 organization surveyed did not yet have a diversity or inclusion "function," and 34% did not have a "specific role for the person in charge of diversity and inclusion," those responsibilities fell to HR or a VP and each year more companies add chief diversity officers or executives to coordinate and accomplish institutional D&I.[148]

Finally, look at your ERGs or Affinity groups as resources for cross-company training, and for information on the success of your fulfillment of diversity and inclusion promises. When allowed to share candid feedback on your company's programs, policies, and products, ERGs can be leading indicators of how well your company is reflecting the needs and wants both of your employees and consumers.

For example, Microsoft uses its 47 employee networks and 7 global employee resource groups to support the careers and networking, community participation and product input. These ERGs also support the company's key initiatives for diversity and inclusion:

- **Recruiting executive talent,** with a strategic and proactive focus on prospecting diverse talent
- **Recognizing and encouraging technical women**
- **Promoting the study of computer science at universities**, specifically by forming partnerships with academic organizations, including traditionally female schools, Historically Black Colleges and Universities and Hispanic-Serving Institutions to develop a strong IT curriculum.
- **Encouraging girls and diverse students to study computing** through their DigiGirlz program, DO-IT (Disabilities, Opportunities, Internetworking and Technology), and Blacks at Microsoft Minority Student Day, to expose diverse high school students to the high-tech work world.
- **Recruiting the best and the brightest**
- **Celebrating what technology can do to empower people**[149]

ESPN, one of the world's leading sports brands, has a very active and progressive LGBT ERG called ESPN Equal. In addition, they launched an employee-based program for allies of the LGBT community to stand up in vocal support of their fellow employees by creating a video with TV personalities to join a new Ally program, "to help foster a workplace at ESPN where lesbian, gay, bisexual and transgender employees are accepted, included and supported."[150] ESPN continues to advocate for LGBT equality "on-air ... (and) behind the scenes." As OutSports.com commends, "they have put their money where their mouth is."

COMPANY CASE STUDY:
Approach to Diversity: MLB

It was unprecedented when Wendy Lewis's position as SVP Diversity and Strategic Alliances, Office of the Commissioner was created by Major League Baseball. She has brought game-changing D&I strategies and metrics to all thirty club franchises, as well as the MLB central office, MLB Advanced Media and the MLB Network, "really looking at workforce diversity," as she says. "And by diversity, I also mean inclusion. It's more than just having more representation of a particular race or women, but making sure that we are working more toward achieving sort of the ultimate balance. We are doing that by taking a real, very strategic and very micro look at each one of those establishments and the pipeline of folks that they actually have coming in."[151]

These efforts are turning around diversity statistics, with the fact that there were 68 African-Americans on opening-day rosters after three decades of decline in representation, according to a study by *USA TODAY Sports*. Ms. Lewis has implemented the lauded and innovative Diversity Economic Impact Engagement (DEIE) model, which the American Advertising Federation describes as "designed to advance League-wide the level of MLB's workforce, supply chain and Club engagement levels of diversity and inclusion leadership and progress."[152] A key aspect of the DEIE is MLB's supplier diversity initiative, the Diverse Business

Partners program, through which Major League Baseball has brought in $1 billion in revenue for women- and minority-owned companies, according to *INSIGHT Into Diversity*[153].

Closest to Lewis's heart, she says, is the MLB Diversity Business Summit, the premier sports employment conference and supplier diversity trade fair. This two-day event allows job seekers and entrepreneurs the unique opportunity of meeting with MLB's Clubs at both the Major League and Minor League levels as well as sponsorship partners.

"We bring together the whole universe of our game in one spot for the sole purpose of creating a phenomenal engagement opportunity around jobs and entrepreneurship for baseball," says Lewis. "All 30 clubs are present, the commissioner is present, 10 of our minor league clubs are present, and we network with a range of job seekers and entrepreneurs. Our objective is to make sure that more people are getting those employment and procurement opportunities. We can't get it done without the commissioner, without the owners, without the clubs being in agreement that a diverse population is in the best interest of the game and our business.

She also implements MLB's Diversity Economic Impact Engagements (DEIE), one of MLB's newest initiatives to advance the level of MLB's current workforce and supplier diversity efforts. She also develops methodologies for cultural assessments, diversity economic platforms and industry-wide diversity training, and she manages MLB's Executive Development Program (EDP) and The Diverse Business Partners Program, the premier supplier diversity program in sports.

Together these efforts advance the progress of diversity and inclusion at Major League Baseball on all levels.

COMPANY CASE STUDY: NASCAR
Drive for Diversity

Each year, the NASCAR Drive for Diversity Initiative seeks the highest quality applicants representing the most diverse backgrounds and develop them into successful NASCAR drivers. It is one of NASCAR's Director of Diversity Affairs and Multicultural Development Dawn Harris's most high-profile and effective efforts to promote the NASCAR brand to a multicultural audience while diversifying from within.

Instituted by the American auto-racing league, the program's purpose is to attract minorities and women to the sport, primarily as drivers, but also to include diverse applicants for ownership, sponsorship, and crew member roles. NASCAR also aims to attract a more diverse audience to the historically white, male-dominated sport. Wikipedia describes the system as similar to a driver development program, where applicants progress through minor-league and regional racing levels to prepare them for a possible shot at one of NASCAR's three national series. Six diverse drivers were selected for the 2016 NASCAR Drive for Diversity® (D4D) class and will join the industry's premier development program for multicultural and female drivers, and pit crew members.[154]

In an additional indication that Harris's efforts are gaining traction, the Africa Channel announced that it would enter a stock car in NASCAR's racing series, and Randy Fenley, a partner in the endeavor, said the announcement signals that the cable television channel is launching a driver-and racing crew-development training program for African Americans to enter the popular sport.[155]

"This is a unique opportunity for an African-American-owned media entity to have a presence in one of America's most popular and dynamic sports," said Eldrick Williams, president and CEO of The Africa Channel to New America Media. "The race car will offer a unique marketing platform, as well as provide opportunities to develop compelling TV content."

According to the NASCAR, which is based in Daytona Beach, Florida, stock car racing is the fastest-growing sport among African-Americans and Hispanics. Since 1995, the percentage of black fans increased 18 percent to 2 million. Hispanic viewership of NASCAR races broadcast on Fox was up 30% from 2012-2013, and about one in ten African Americans state that they have watched at least one NASCAR race in the past twelve months.[156]

"Large urban markets have a significant number of households tuning in each week to each NASCAR Events," NASCAR said. Steve Tullman, co-owner of Tullman/Fenley Motorsports and a leader in the biotech industry, also sees the NASCAR initiative as a platform to raise awareness about serious health issues, including diabetes, heart disease and cancer, which are chronic among African Americans.

"This relationship is the catalyst for dramatic progress in the efforts to bring true diversity to the incredible sport of NASCAR. The partnership brings exposure to potential fans not normally engaged in NASCAR, while at the same time providing opportunities for very talented drivers who have yet been able to showcase their talents," Fenley said.

"NASCAR remains steadfast in its mission to develop multicultural and female athletes, and we believe this (2016) class has the potential to compete at the highest levels of our sport," said Jim Cassidy, NASCAR senior vice president of racing operations. "The talent pool from which these drivers were selected was unprecedented for NASCAR Drive for Diversity–a testament to the program's growth and success."

NewAmericanMedia.org

CHAPTER 5

DASHBOARD/SCORECARD

EFFECTIVE D&I EFFORTS have clear goals and measureable outcomes. These goals and outcomes in turn outline the critical steps necessary for your business success. Developing a D&I Scorecard in order to measure your efforts in various business areas **will** demonstrate the ways in which your D&I strategy is working, plus give you the metrics to prove its impact on corporate business objectives. You will also find that these concrete, quantified terms support your arguments for funding future D&I efforts in a systematic and innovative way. You will be able to demonstrate the ways in which your Big Six D&I framework build business value and contribute to your bottom-line.

As former Cisco VP of Corporate Quality Rich Goldberg reminds us, "Metrics and measurements are essential elements to driving change and raising visibility around the business value resulting from inclusion and diversity.

Metrics provide a common language we can understand and agree upon. Measurements give an objective perspective, allowing us to more easily spot, analyze, and then ultimately address problems. The focus is on the problem, instead of specific behaviors or people."[157]

Dashboards and scorecards are analytical tools that allow you to highlight the measurements that are important to your business. The idea behind them is to provide you and your top executives with a customizable view of key performance indicators (KPIs) that give you actionable information. Some companies or D&I departments develop a **dashboard** as a data visualization tool that displays the current status of your enterprise's metrics and results; it tends to be more focused on specific operational goals & objectives, while **scorecards** ensure that a business remains focused on organizational strategies in monitoring performance execution and mapping results against defined strategies over time.

Dashboards consolidate and arrange numbers, metrics and sometimes performance scorecards on a single screen. Like the dashboard of a car, dashboards traditionally indicate the status at a specific point in time, whereas a scorecard displays progress towards set goals over time, and compares strategic goals with results.[158]

DASHBOARD	SCORECARD
Tactical - focused on short-term decision making.	Strategic - focused on long-term decision making.
Provides a snapshot of business performance.	Represents trends/changes in business activity over time.
Operationally focused and supported by individual managers.	Supported by clearly defined management strategy.
Change in performance evaluated by primary decision-makers/ stakeholders.	Changes in performance measured against business goals.

159

Dashboard and scorecard designs are increasingly converging (products combining elements of both are sometimes referred to as a "scoreboard!"); some performance management articles use the words interchangeably, as though there is no longer really a distinction between them. So I'm going to describe the key elements of a Diversity Scorecard Framework; you can research various commercial tools or develop one that is customized to your needs and data sets. The crucial idea is to use these tools to move beyond the simple measurement or monitoring provided by metrics, and instead to actively manage towards defined goals. Managing your D&I performance requires integrating goals, programs, and metrics.

The most effective metrics take a holistic approach to the measurement process. I advocate that you assess the impact of your Diversity and Inclusion strategies across multiple platforms: Workforce, Workplace, Community, and Marketplace. In each of these four business areas, you will identify the right tools to measure your D&I efforts' effectiveness, both efficiently and accurately. Each area needs to be connected to clear and specific goals, which derive from your goal-setting stage in the Big Six. Without them, there can be no gauge of progress.

As we've all heard, "What gets measured gets done." It also gets funded, supported, and respected. You want to use measurement and scoreboard strategies in order to solidify the role of D&I within your company's values and priorities.

I also encourage you to begin NOW. This may sound scary—perhaps embarrassing, confusing, premature—but do it!

Take a snapshot of your D&I benchmarks even if you have not yet begun to develop D&I strategies, metrics, and goals. It is bound to yield a great deal of data in those four categories. As Michele Meyer-Shipp, Vice-President and Chief Diversity Officer at Prudential Financial discovered, even the questions that she and her team could *not* answer, at first, yielded valuable information about how to establish definitions, goals, and diversity priorities in her company's next months and years. But it was clear that "D&I is integral to the strength of our talent, culture, business performance and identity" and "diverse vantage points lead to success in the workplace, marketplace and community."[160] Measurements could only help quantify this success and direct next steps to achieving it.

Once you take this look at where you are, in time, you actually *have a benchmark* from which to improve and grow.

Diversity & Inclusion Scorecard Framework

Here is a way to develop your own D&I Scorecard, by considering the following 6 steps as a guide to your process. I'll then look at ways to develop valuable measurements in those four strategic areas of your business.

A. **Identify** what your organization accomplished last year, where it's headed next year, and what budget is needed both to do a thorough measurement as well realize your diversity objectives.

B. **Objectives** of your scorecards are, first, to establish a baseline so that you know where you are and what you'd like to change. Second, use your scorecard development to ensure that your D&I goals are specific and definable, plus measurable, and that you have a fix on who are the accountable parties for each element.

C. **Planning** involves listing your annual goals as developed from your baseline and how it is that you are going to change it.

D. **Management accountability,** as I discuss in more detail below, is critical to your D&I strategy success. So, in your framework stage, identify ways to link your goals and objectives to select bonuses or incentive programs in order to enhance management buy-in.

E. **Workforce levels detail** is going to help you as you begin to develop scorecards for your human assets. Before progress can be made in your talent diversity efforts, you'll need to have complete detail on the demographics of your VPs, managers, SVPs, etc.

F. Compliance, EEO, & Affirmative Action also impact your needs and objectives, so you'll check both your baselines and your goals implementation against any concerns you have about either internal or external compliance, or any ways that you can support corporate initiatives through affirmative action.[161]

#1—Workforce

What are the leading indicators that you want to measure in your analysis of your workforce, now and moving forward? Broadly speaking, as regards to the talent management of your diverse target populations and as compared to non-minority men, these should include:

- ➤ Recruitment
- ➤ Hiring representation
- ➤ Movement--both promotions & lateral
- ➤ Retention vs. attrition & turnover
- ➤ Talent assessments & leadership development, competency gaps; and
- ➤ Corporate Engagement

At Walmart, the Office of Diversity does two major types of workforce measurement. The first is done quarterly (see below about using these reports to structure and evaluate goals) and looks at "representations." This scorecard analyzes the demographic facts within Walmart's various business units, then who has been promoted broken down by diverse groups, who may have been demoted, and who left the company. Performance reviews on all levels are translated, in part, into metrics, so that the Scorecard report also charts those who were rated as exceeding expectations and those who rated as below, again matched to the company's demographics. Walmart senior director of global diversity Donald Fan finds these scorecards extremely useful in painting a picture, for himself and senior managers, as to what is going on within the company.

The second direct measure that his office takes annually is an opinion survey across all of Walmart's associates. It focuses on their engagement rate, and can also be used as a tool to define and review diversity & inclusion goals. Ernst & Young calls this their "global people survey." It also includes some demographic information including sexual orientation, abled or not, etc., so that the data can be used for representation purposes as well; but, in addition, it includes a broad set of questions regarding inclusiveness.

By marrying the two sets of information together or looking at the demographic components of Ernst & Young's surveys, you can discover that different perceptions often translate into different experiences for certain of your demographic groups. This might suggest to you specific new actions for that group.

For example, as Jim Norman, the former VP of Diversity for Kraft Foods, explained about his engagement questionnaires, "If I were looking through the engagement survey data and, for example, I saw that women of color responded very differently and were less favorable than people of color in general, and I saw that African-American women felt rated the lowest across all dimensions, I could then correlate across all dimensions and retrace my turnover rates and promotion rates and representation rates for women of color, specifically African Americans. It adds texture to the data as I'm trying to build a story for strategy and action. They don't have to be present; I can use their collective voices."[162]

When you design your own workforce analysis, consider your total addressable market, like Cisco Systems does in their Business Stakeholder Review. For example, when you look at hiring as a significant part of your D&I pipeline, measure first how many opportunities there were to hire across the company or within a given division, that year. Then how many applicants you attracted from within your target demographic groups (e.g., women, minorities, sexual orientation, alternately abled). Then quantify how many interviews by category and how many offers tendered. This is richer, more actionable information than just who joins or leaves your company.

When you are looking to hire a reflective labor pool within a given location or division, consider taking your national business data as it relates to hiring or representation and overlay it geographically. ADP chief diversity officer Rita Mitjans found anomalies, for example, in their Hispanic hiring in a part of the country with a large employable Hispanic talent pool. Although they wanted to hire a representative group of employees, "we weren't good at it yet," she discovered.

Expanding your human talent metrics in this way gives you a full-lens look at the talent acquisition and management process. And continue to expand that lens. While 77% of companies have annual targets for race or ethnicity and 71% for gender, as ways of increasing diversity from within, "less common are quotas based on gender identity (3%), religious affiliation (2%) or familial status (1%)" and only 41% of organizations surveyed in late 2015 had targets for veterans.[163]

Ultimately, as your data establishes benchmarks and indicates trending, you will be able to design and revise your D&I priorities much more concretely, and then create results. As Jim Norman went on to say, "the actions you take in closing the gap for the general population may not work for underrepresented groups ... Take your data and look at it through the responses of the underrepresented groups."[164] Then begin to design goals to move the needle in critical areas of under-representation or slow improvement.

As Michelle Winterspoon, former Inclusion and Diversity Manager at Cisco explained, her department did their analysis to identify gaps, and then presented this customized diversity intelligence to her senior management in order to **use the metrics to inspire action.** Her strategy did not involve sending over a report and waiting for a response. Cisco executives had to meet with the Diversity chief and have an open conversation about it, first. She limited the participants in these discussions, and did not let the EVPs or SVPs keep the data after their meeting together. In response, however, they were required to put an action plan together within sixty days of reviewing the report, and propose specific ways to address the organization's major gaps over the next year. These became the next year's scorecard targets.

At the same time as she gave them the company-wide data reports, themselves, Winterspoon provided insight into Cisco's representational and inclusion information by sharing with her senior executives trending demographics for the company's areas of business. She extracted the inclusion pulse index scores from her associates' surveys and compares those against outside benchmarking reports like those made available by DiversityBestPractices.com.

This additional intelligence provided perspective and allowed her senior management to prioritize their D&I goals for the coming year in a more holistic way.

The Coca Cola Company has three parts to their annual diversity report, and the below infographics give a nice visual representation of the company's U.S. workforce in this sample Benchmark Report.

Walgreens created an infographic to reflect their D&I Vision statement and then the Accountability and Assessment Measurements they do.

TOTAL U.S. WORKFORCE:
12/31/14

BY GENDER

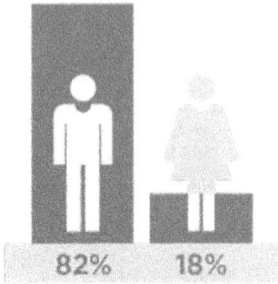

82%   18%

BY RACE

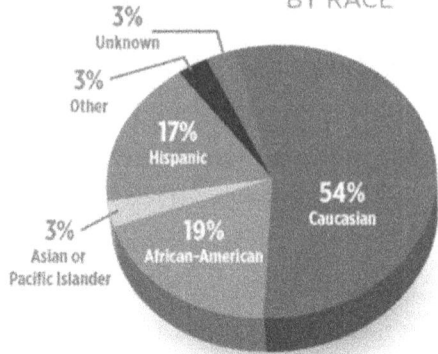

3% Unknown

3% Other

17% Hispanic

3% Asian or Pacific Islander

19% African-American

54% Caucasian

TOTAL U.S. CORPORATE HEADQUARTERS WORKFORCE:
12/31/14

BY GENDER

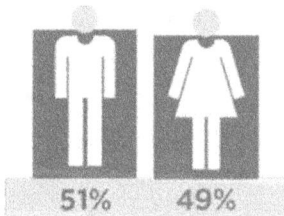

51%   49%

BY RACE

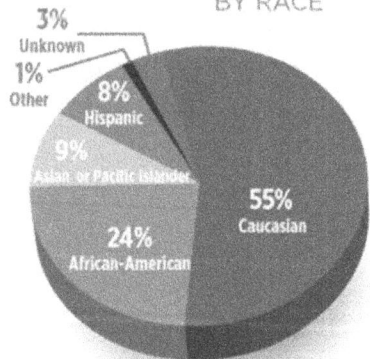

3% Unknown

1% Other

8% Hispanic

9% Asian or Pacific Islander

24% African-American

55% Caucasian

TOTAL U.S. WORKFORCE, COCA-COLA REFRESHMENTS & COCA-COLA NORTH AMERICA:
12/31/14

BY GENDER   BY RACE

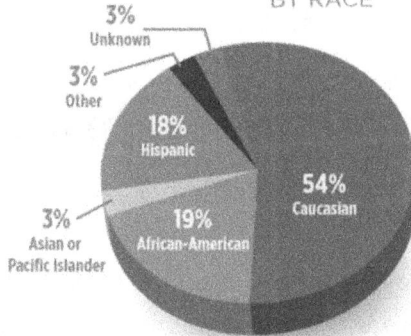

Sample Workforce Diversity Benchmark Report :
The Coca Cola Company, 2015

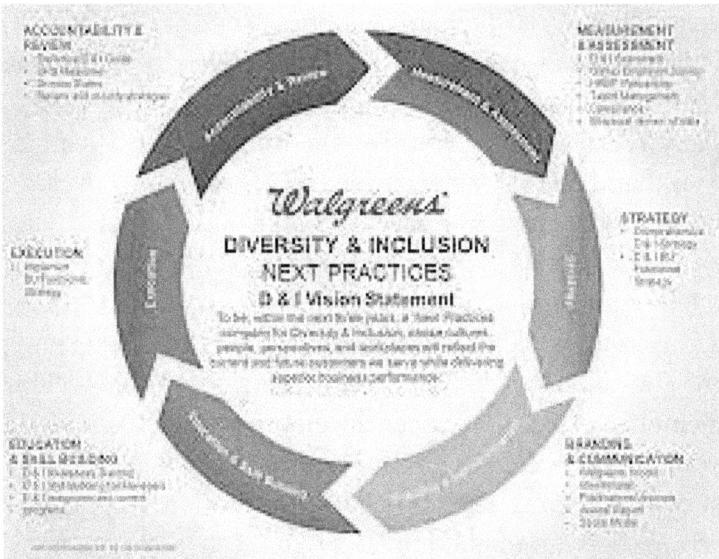

Walgreens D&I "Accountability & Review" © 2010 Walgreens Co.

COMPANY CASE STUDY
SODEXO

Sodexo is a worldwide leader in delivering services to organizations interested in improving the quality of life for their employees, from their health and well-being to benefits and rewards services, personal and home services. The company operates in eighty countries, where the company's almost 419,000 employees interact with over 75 million customers each day.

According to *Diversity Global Magazine*, one of the challenges Sodexo has met is to embed diversity and inclusion (D&I) principles into their human resources practices. The company relies on top executive Dr. Rohini Anand, senior vice president and global chief diversity officer, to "develop and implement a holistic D&I approach that is based on standardized values and principles but with localized implementation of day-to-day talent management practices."

Dr. Anand explains that Sodexo is a decentralized company, so, in and outside the U.S., key metrics around retention, engagement, promotion, and development are used to keep everyone onboard with D&I. Sodexo uses a scorecard that measures recruiting, retention, and promotion of women and minorities. Measurement is one of the Ten Key Elements for

Inclusion and Systemic Culture Change that they use to integrate D&I into the Sodexo corporate culture.

These are:

1) Integrate Diversity & Inclusion into All Functions and Core Business Strategy
2) Commitment From the Top
3) Strong Business Case
4) Clearly Articulated Diversity Strategy
5) Resources & Structure
6) Grassroots Involvement
7) Measurement Systems
8) Accountability
9) Strong Supplier Diversity & Partnerships
10) Internal & External Recognition

As part of their measurement and accountability process, Sodexo has developed a highly regarded Diversity Scorecard that reports progress on what Dr. Anand terms the Sodexo Diversity Index (SDI) to leadership on a monthly basis.

The Sodexo Diversity Index (SDI) Components actually constitute a formula for that company's success:

The **Quantitative** elements (which include *Hiring, Promotions* and *Retention)* are added to the **Qualitative** elements (comprised of *Supplier Diversity, Engagement and Involvement, Diversity Training, Mentoring*, and the *monitoring of minority and women high potentials)*. Together, these "equal" the Sodexo Diversity Index, by summarizing the weighted Quantitative and Qualitative results into one comprehensive "score."

Sodexo calibrates the weighting of their index formula annually, which helps them to reinforce their focus on meeting the company's D&I targets, which Dr. Anand developed in association with her team, the international division, and HR leaders company-wide, and which helps management see how D&I is meeting the developing needs of their organization.

Sodexo also has developed a concrete financial accountability structure to link together with its D&I mission and scorecard metrics.

Their Diversity Scorecard is a strategic measurement tool used to measure corporate progress in meeting the company's stated D&I strategies and in increasing D&I in their management positions.

There are two aspects to this scorecard: **Development,** which includes industry best practices, input from their divisions to attain buy-in throughout all their business units, annual recalibration to check that their measurements are relevant and also having positive impact on the outcomes they seek to attain, and the *qualitative* and *quantitative* measures mentioned above, which look at staff efforts around things like retention and recruitment to advance diversity and inclusion; and **Application,** which involves monthly monitoring by senior management, scorecards that are tailored to various business or enterprise units specifically, and a two-tier analysis of recruitment and retention, both of *senior leaders* and *entry and middle management* positions.

There is also a financial system in place for Scorecard Accountability: 25% of all Sodexo executive team bonuses are connected to the performance of the SDI; and 10-15% of management bonuses (senior and mid-level managers) relate to Diversity Scorecard performance. Furthermore, the company is committed to paying on these successes regardless of the company's financial performance.[165]

#2—Workplace

You want to design ways to measure the improvements that your D&I initiatives have brought into your workplace and identify gaps or needs that can promote diversity throughout your corporate culture. There are numerous goals and objectives that you may establish in order to encourage diversity in the promotions that occur in your business, from mentoring to professional development to educational engagement. The success of your diversity & inclusion goals will always begin with great leadership and policies, but you also need to measure the ways in which these are put into practice throughout your company, and ensure that they are executed by the managers responsible for a given business unit.

Since your objective is to build an inclusive culture that seeks to recruit, retain, and promote diverse individuals, you need to assess baseline strengths and areas for improvement related to your inclusion and diversity efforts. Then, determine progress towards inclusions goals in your institutional diversity plan.

Interestingly, high performing companies and organizations that have an increasingly diverse talent pool have shown that, in market economies, talented workers from diverse backgrounds have similar baseline needs that must be met by winning companies (and that are also comparable to those of non-diverse male workers). Studies conducted by the Gallup organization indicate that there are clear satisfiers and dissatisfiers for employees across industries and demographic distinctions.

The **satisfiers** include:

- Getting to do what I do best
- Caring managers and supervisors
- Positive co-worker relationships
- Adequate resources to do my job
- Trust and treatment by upper management
- Opportunities to learn and grow
- Clear expectations about the work requirements
- Competitive compensation, reward, and recognition

The **dissatisfiers** include:

- Prejudice and discrimination for arbitrary reasons
- Poor career development opportunity
- Poor work environment or climate
- Low organizational savvy on the people issues
- Pressure to conform or assimilate[166]

The bottom line is that **Engagement Creates Better Performance.** Companies that promote a culture that produces these satisfiers and eliminates the dissatisfiers produce better results.

What's the positive differential between companies that are effective at creating inclusion and companies that are not?

- **Customer satisfaction +39%**
- **Productivity +22%**
- **Profitability +27%**
- **Lower turnover -22%**

—Source: Cumulative Gallup Workplace Studies

So, you need to take a regular pulse on your company culture and how well your diverse employees are engaged. 87% of C-Suite executives recognize that disengaged employees represent one of the biggest threats to their business.[167]

How can you measure your employee engagement? Ideally, you will develop a tool to measure your institutional climate and culture through the lens of diversity and inclusion. This can be based on traditional engagement analytics (see below) that you either enhance or, as Jim Norman described above, that you analyze through your D&I lens.

One reliable basic instrument is Gallup's "G12 feedback system," based on the factors that determine both active engagement and disengagement. Their research (which consistently shows a correlation between high survey scores and superior job performance) developed this series of questions, which are rated on a scale from one to five:

1. Do I know what is expected of me at work?

2. Do I have the materials and equipment that I need in order to do my work right?

3. At work, do I have the opportunity to do what I do best every day?

4. In the last seven days, have I received recognition or praise for doing good work?

5. Does my supervisor, or someone at work, seem to care about me as a person?

6. Is there someone at work who encourages my development?

7. At work, do my opinions seem to count?

8. Does the mission or purpose of my company make me feel that my job is important?

9. Are my coworkers committed to doing quality work?

10. Do I have a best friend at work?

11. In the past six months, has someone at work talked to me about my progress?

12. This past year, have I had opportunities at work to learn and grow?[168]

For smaller workplaces, you may not need to do broad polling in order to assess your employee engagement effectively. One-on-one meetings with employees might do the trick. At medium and larger workplaces, you may want to supplement one-on-one meetings with town hall meetings, focus groups, and/or surveys. One key to success, however, is to be sure that you ask all employees the same questions. This will permit you to analyze your feedback better, and design more targeted action steps, as a consequence.

Another leader in building science-based tools to measure and manage employee engagement, loyalty and retention, is Quantum Workplace. They have developed slightly different survey questions to assess employee engagement, asking that the following statements be ranked on a scale of one to ten.[169]

1. Management provides good leadership and guidance during difficult economic conditions.

2. My job is mentally stimulating.

3. I understand how my work contributes to my company's performance.

4. There are future opportunities for growth at my company.

5. My company affords me the opportunity to develop my skills.

6. I receive recognition and reward for my contributions.

7. There is open, honest communication between employees and managers.

8. I see professional growth and career opportunities for myself in this organization.

9. I know how I fit into the organization's future plans.

10. Considering the value I bring to the organization, I am paid fairly.

In your efforts to give a voice to diverse populations and to gather a snapshot of your employees' attitudes towards diversity and inclusion, develop ways to identify salient concerns such as historical baggage from stereotypes, social isolation, economic constraints, and the impact of your most culturally competent role models and mentors on demographic groups within your organization.

Again, you are going to use this data to help you formulate and further your action plans and goals.

For this part of his institutional surveying, Kraft's Jim Norman relied heavily on his employee resource groups. And he utilized ERGs not just to gauge employee engagement, but to make organizational initiatives successful. By holding Kraft's ERGs responsible for various benchmarks after taking an annual pulse and setting new targets, Norman enhanced the buy-in of Kraft's employees to the company's objectives and priorities.

Cigna similarly relies on Employee-led Colleague Resource Groups (CRGs) to measure and then develop initiatives around understanding the particular needs of their customer segments, according to their Chief Diversity Officer Rosanna Duruthy.[170]

Diversity & Inclusion Training is most effective when it is part of a strategy focused on improving business results. Ideally, your diversity training should achieve certain workforce and work environment changes that will help meet your business objectives, which may include developing new knowledge, skills, experiences, or action plans. Your Diversity and Inclusion training program should inform people about the organization's business needs, what changes need to be implemented in order to grow the business, and it should provide specific knowledge, skills, and tools that people can use in their daily work. In addition, you want these programs to focus on developing people's intercultural expertise in leading, working in, and contributing to the success of your increasingly diverse and multicultural organization.

There are many books available on how to develop, conduct, and follow up on diversity and inclusion trainings, including ways to define your learning outcomes. But, in keeping with the spirit of my thesis here, I believe that it is incumbent on you to define the business goals that your trainings are intended to help achieve. Once you have identified what changes are needed in the workforce ("who we are") and/or the workplace ("how we work together") to help meet your business goals, you want to articulate how your D&I trainings will help make the needed workforce and/or workplace changes. Always share how given trainings fit into your overall D&I strategy. Then, determine how you plan to measure the results, in terms that are meaningful to your senior leadership.

As part of your workplace evaluations, develop measurable data for your trainings, and include this information in your scorecards or dashboard. Include the number of supervisors, managers, and employees who receive diversity and inclusion training each fiscal year, and/or the percent of managers that complete any Diversity & Inclusion annual diversity training requirement, if you have one. Devise a training evaluation that permits participants to indicate their increased understanding of diversity and inclusion principles.

Calculate the number of diversity-related activities and events that are initiated or sponsored by your senior leaders and supervisors/managers. Consider developing a simple reporting tool that helps them to document diversity and inclusion activities and events.

You may want to measure the percent improvement in your employee surveys around their assessment that things like creativity and innovation are rewarded; or that policies and programs promote D&I in the workplace; that managers, supervisors, and team leaders work well with employees of different backgrounds; and that their supervisor/team leader is committed to a workforce that is representative of all segments of society.

Consider ways that you can promote the successes that you observe, or develop D&I awards that tie to meeting various benchmarks, and which recognize managers/supervisors, executives, and non-supervisors who support innovative approaches to improving your workforce diversity, and to creating an inclusive workplace environment. Design a process by which managers are recognized and rewarded for their efforts to promote diversity and inclusion activities and events.

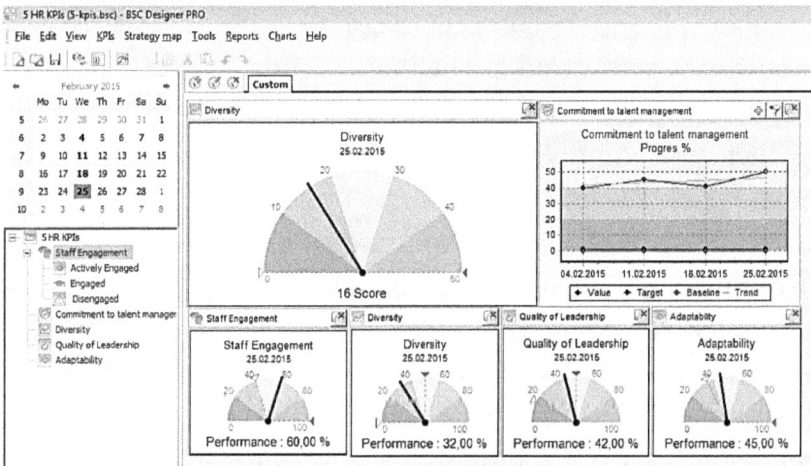

Sample Dashboard[171]

#3—Community

Each of your goals and initiatives directed at diversifying your community outreach, and designed to impact the multicultural communities and target groups that you identified in your D&I strategy can be tied to a set of benchmarks, measurements, and metrics. You want to find ways to measure community benefits as you enhance your community relations. In addition to your quantitative scorecards, you can include qualitative measurements through engaging community constituents and garnering feedback.

How many diverse community organizations have you partnered with? What numbers do their constituencies represent? How many impressions for your company have been made in diverse communities? How many scholarships given? Or internships, or gifts and donations made to community efforts that impact these constituencies? How many of your company employees are involved in community organizations or events? Design, support, and encourage outreach opportunities for every level of employee, from volunteer and matching gift opportunities, to positions on non-profit boards of directors.

Lockheed Martin Corp has long supported LGBT inclusion and founded a dedicated ERG, PRIDE, in 1981. Not only does this organization offer LGBT employees and straight allies the opportunity to "seek ways to shape the future together," just as the company's scientists "see the world and seek to understand it," but PRIDE members "mentor youth and encourage them to pursue careers in science, technology, engineering and mathematics. The company also sponsors Out in STEM or oSTEM Inc., OUT for Work, transgender career fairs and OUT to Innovate™" as ways to grow new LGBT professionals as well as reach out to their customer communities.[172] Lockheed Martin quantifies membership in PRIDE in the thousands and celebrates the ERG's "tremendous impact on people's lives internally and externally through mentoring, outreach and education."

In many instances, your company now looks to measure their Return on Investment for philanthropic and community involvement. And there are both tangible and intangible benefits to these efforts. But consider what does an ROI look like on your diversity initiatives within the community? And how can you use these measurements to enhance sales, increase customer retention, and improve or expand your company's media/image?

Certainly calculate media mentions and awards, plus survey awareness levels of your diversity message external to your company.

The Coca-Cola Company, for example, considers one measurement of their commitment to diversity to be how they are seen through the eyes of others. When they paint their diversity picture, they foreground the facts that for ten consecutive years, they have received a top rating of 100 percent from the Human Rights Campaign for their performance regarding workplace policies for lesbian, gay, bisexual and transgender associates and the Coca-Cola Company became the first company to feature a same-gender couple in a Super Bowl ad when its "It's Beautiful" spot ran during the second quarter of the 2014 game; they received the 2013 Catalyst Award in recognition of their work to advance and empower women in the workplace and across their value chain and the December 2014 HACR (Hispanic Association on Corporate Responsibility) Corporate Inclusion Index rating of 90 (December 2014);

and ranked for twelve years on DiversityInc.'s Top 50 Companies.[173]

Cigna's Hispanic-Latino CRG developed a white paper entitled "'America's Hispanic Community,' centered on the Hispanic concept of *bienestar*—a state of deep well-being derived from the interrelationship between family, community, and good health. The white paper highlights opportunities to improve health outcomes and how to create a deeper engagement with America's Hispanic employees."[174] The CRG also created a video series, and, together, the white paper and videos directly interface with Cigna's community and demonstrate how the company "uses its unique abilities to bring together multiple perspectives, backgrounds, cultures, and skills."

#4—Marketplace

Your diversity analytics are just as important when applied to your company's marketplace as they are to your internal talent resource management. The ultimate proof of your D&I success is going to be demonstrated in business bottom line reports. You want to develop benchmarks and scorecards that define diversity goals for your corporate sales, customer acquisition, and customer retention, as mapped against your target groups.

Once you have activated your efforts at diversifying your markets, you will want to include benchmarks and calculations for new sales in targeted markets, and calculate changes in incremental revenues. Consider enlisting your ERGs in these efforts, and then match sales data against periods that did not have ERG support.

Monitor overall profitability and incremental revenues in your diversity sales throughout scorecard periods in order to generate measurements of diversity sales retention, as well. When you undertake target marketing, survey attendance and demographics of attendees throughout regular intervals of your event, then compare pre- and post-event sales or sales of prior years.

Furthermore, everything that I discussed in terms of Supplier Diversity should be tied to scorecards and metrics. Include not only numbers of suppliers and their regions, but what percentage of your company's total spending is attributable to spending at diverse suppliers. This will give you concrete evidence of how your policies have impact, and establish new benchmarks and targets upon which to improve.

Walmart quantifies their women-owned-business supplier diversity statistics below, then also lays out in an infographic their approach to general supplier diversity and some additional metrics:

Aspiration: *Double sourcing from WOBs in our international markets through 2016.*

We've calculated the baseline spend on WOBs in seven markets, tracked quarterly progress toward the goal and have begun to implement tailored strategies by market to grow spend. In five tracked international markets, Walmart has increased annual spend among women by more than 21 percent from FYE12 to FYE15.

5-year total women-owned supplier spend – $20 billion commitment

(amounts in billions)

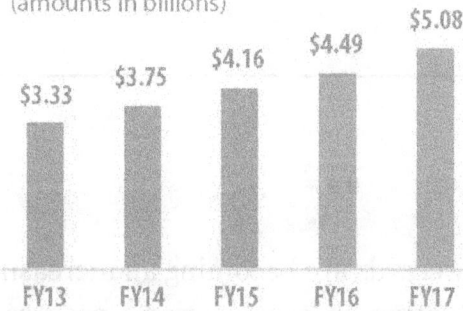

FY13	FY14	FY15	FY16	FY17
$3.33	$3.75	$4.16	$4.49	$5.08

■ $11.24 billion – Achieved
($775 million ahead of goal to date)

■ $8.76 billion – Remaining goal

*FYE15 = Feb.1, 2014 -Jan 31,2015

BUSINESS INTEGRATION

Supplier diversity

At Walmart, we believe we're at our best when we promote diversity across our supply chain. For us, supplier diversity means delivering better products and a broader selection to the communities we serve. Through our supplier diversity efforts, we're committed to creating economic growth and sustainable communities by:

- Increasing sourcing from businesses owned by people of diverse backgrounds, including minorities, women and people with disabilities

- Fostering an inclusive supply chain that's relevant to our customers and meets their needs

IN 2014

SPENT WITH DIVERSE SUPPLIERS

$13.5 Billion

DIRECT SPENDING

$10.4 Billion

SECOND-TIER SPENDING

$3.1 Billion

SPENT WITH WOMEN-OWNED BUSINESSES

$4.16 Billion

Supporting supplier diversity

SUPPLIER DIVERSITY SUMMIT

Each year, our Supplier Diversity Summit serves as an opportunity for suppliers and our buyers to engage. The purpose of the summit is to:

- Advise, advocate and advance dialogue between diverse businesses and the internal stakeholders that will help our customers save money and live better

- Help potential suppliers understand our EDLC & EDLP strategy

- Create the opportunity for suppliers to present their products to our buyers

- Engage our buyers to leverage the insights, innovation and expertise of diverse suppliers

- Perpetuate the impact of diverse businesses in the communities we serve

COLLABORATION

We support and collaborate with leading organizations that advocate on behalf of diversity-owned businesses. These partnerships include:

- National Minority Supplier Development Council
- US Black Chambers, Inc.
- U.S. Pan Asian American Chamber of Commerce
- U.S. Business Leadership Network (USBLN) Disability Supplier Diversity Program (DSDP)
- WBENC International
- The Latino Coalition

- U.S. Department of Veterans Affairs Center for Veterans Enterprise
- Women's Business Enterprise National Council
- National Center for American Indian Enterprise Development
- National Asian/Pacific Islander American Chamber of Commerce & Entrepreneurship
- National Veteran-Owned Business Association

175

###

While diversity scorecards are becoming an increasingly important tool in evaluating an organization's progress in diversity and inclusion, the specific components of a particular scorecard can vary greatly. However, the most effective metrics include a holistic approach to the process and assess the impact of diversity and inclusion across multiple platforms, such as market share, suppliers, workforce, and customers.

Cold, hard data is hard to ignore. When you can credibly show a business leader that current conditions are not going to take them where they need to go, you make that leader your partner in driving change. Measurements enable you to create accountability and establish a baseline by which success or opportunities for improvement can be quantified. They also give you the ability to quantify the value to be derived from diversity and inclusion as you raise the visibility of changing demographic issues, and create links between them and overall business performance.

COMPANY CASE STUDY
MasterCard: Diversity & Inclusion as Business Imperatives

Through a combination of policies and metrics, MasterCard Chief Diversity Officer Donna Johnson and her team have "built a culture that develops (their) employees professionally a d personally, making MasterCard a fantastic place to work."[176]

The company sees diversity and inclusion as key to achieving the innovative MasterCard vision of "A World Beyond Cash."

"MasterCard leverages the unique perspectives of our employees to deliver innovative products and solutions that are as diverse as the consumers we serve around the world. Our inclusive culture is about more than simply having a diverse workforce. It's about using diversity to drive real business impact," explains Tim Murphy, General Counsel and Chief Franchise Officer. "We want our employees to know they're making a real difference when they bring different ways of thinking to the table."

The company has built Shareholder Value on a foundation of Diversity & Inclusion, which is engrained in the company identity. Their inclusive culture is created through:

- **Diversity and Inclusion Strategy:** A culture of diversity and inclusion that increases engagement, innovation and productivity supports our strategic pillars.

- **Global Diversity And Inclusion Council (GDIC):** Senior leaders from our business units drive the diversity and inclusion agenda and strategy.
- **Chief Diversity Officer:** A senior management level position responsible for development and implementation of the diversity and inclusion strategy.
- **Global Diversity Office:** Ensures the principles of diversity and inclusion are embedded throughout the company.
- **Business Resource Groups (BRGs):** Act as internal business consultants to provide consumer segmentation, research, cultural insights and access to networks.
- **Supplier Diversity Program:** Offers opportunities to minority-, women-, disabled- and veteran-owned businesses, and to small businesses as suppliers of our goods and services.

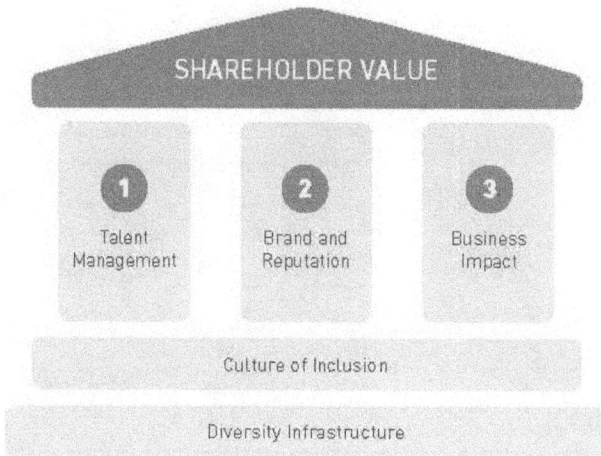

SHAREHOLDER VALUE

1	2	3
Talent Management	Brand and Reputation	Business Impact

Culture of Inclusion

Diversity Infrastructure

Each of these is designed to be measurable, as are their eight Business Research Groups (BRGs) with over 4,000 employees worldwide, which "tap into employee diversity for market insights."

MasterCard also formed the Center for Inclusive Growth to advance sustainable economic growth and financial inclusion around the world. The Center's two focuses are research and global philanthropy, with five major philanthropic initiatives which concentrate on helping global women and youth.[177]

CHAPTER 6:

SUMMARY & CONCLUSION

WE ARE ALL FAMILIAR with the idea behind Sir Richard Branson's maxim, "Doing good is good for business." And clearly, developing a diverse and inclusive workforce, customer base, and supplier network are both good and right things to do. What I also guarantee is that doing Diversity and Inclusion well is your key to great business.

As founder and Chief Learning Executive of Cook Ross says, "The business ROI equation for diversity includes greater innovation, increased work performance, greater job satisfaction and more engaged employees, lower human resources costs, better customer service and wider and deeper market penetration, which equal success at every level at which it can be measured. What more of a business case is necessary to encourage leaders to devote time and resources to creating a more inclusive and culturally competent organizational culture?"[178]

Diversity and Inclusion are the **New Normal** for corporations and institutions. Your charge is to ensure that D&I becomes a key business strategy for your company or association. And framing diversity and inclusion in concrete, business-centered ways are the tools to your company's embracing and progressing them

"Unless we start addressing diversity in these very real, hard, business-centered ways, diversity and inclusion is going to continue to be little more than the theme of a company cocktail party," Tapia says.

Neglecting to tie business and diversity together, or "not grounding diversity in a real way," renders most initiatives superficial and, eventually, useless. When a CEO says, "Diversity is vital to our organization," that's great, but what will it look like put into action? I know that you can follow the proven strategy, my Big Six, in order to ensure success, generate an accurate review of your diversity status, inspire discussion, planning, and implementation, and make it happen in a meaningful way. I am certain that, once you embrace the Big Six and follow the steps and strategies outlined, you too will see the great ways that they contribute directly to your profit centers and bottom line.

ACKNOWLEDGMENTS

FOR AS LONG AS I can remember, there have been a countless number of people that have helped me, and I thank them all.

Some who deserve special mention are as follows:

Mom (Florence P. Abrams)—Your unconditional love and support, as well as guidance, has provided me with the confidence and tools to pursue my dreams.

Dad (Bedford Abrams)—You gave me the greatest gift ever, the desire to never stop learning! As you look down from heaven, I hope that you are proud of the man that I have become.

Chadrick T. Davis and Davita A. Abrams (son and daughter)—While your time on this earth was brief, your presence will always be felt. Thank you for the lifelong memories.

David Anthony Abrams (aka Little D.A.)—Being a proud dad is so easy with you as my son. Thanks for being equally nice and kind as you are smart.

Sisters (Diane Abrams & Bernadette Abrams-Torrance)—Whether it was taking me to karate school on the weekends, driving me to tennis practice at 6AM on

Saturdays, or just simply letting me tag-along, you have always been there for me. You are the best sisters that a little brother could have.

Charnell Abrams, Aqueelah Torrance Johnson, and Allen Torrance (nieces and nephew)—You make it easy to be a proud uncle. You are all so incredible! You are setting a fine example for Little D.A.

Rev. William Pinkney (Uncle Willie)—aka: Real Estate Investor, Business Owner (Two Cleaners), Sharp Dresser, Leader of the Extended Family—May your legacy live forever through the family members you have touched and continue to touch.

Tennis coach, mentor, and advisor Bill Johnson—You believed in me when I did not know how to believe in myself. I am forever grateful for the life-lessons you taught me, on and off the tennis court.

Chris and Leif Beck (founders, NJTL of Philadelphia)— Thank you for bringing tennis (a sport for a lifetime) to North Philly, and throughout the city of Philadelphia. You provided a gateway to many opportunities through tennis.

Henry Michael Williams (cousin and best friend)—You have stood beside me in the toughest of times. And, we have share some unforgettable moments too (all good).

Jim Phipps and John Wylie (best friends)—We met as kids via the NJTL of Philadelphia, and have been the best of friends since the very beginning. I cannot picture life without you in it.

Derrick Lenny Alford (lifelong friend)—I think that we met when we were in diapers. You have been a role model for me since childhood, and you continue to serve as a positive influence in my life.

Greg Williams (lifelong friend)—While I was introduced to tennis by my sister Bernadette, you taught me how to love the sport. You were always an inspiration to me. I continue to cherish my tennis experience, and it is largely because of you.

Chris Stokes (lifelong friend)—You've been my practice partner and friend since 1976, when we both first joined the Mander Playground NJTL tennis team. I'll always remember our being elevated quickly to intermediate level, and a lot of great times, even though we were (unfortunately) also winless for the entire year!

Mike Kennedy (life-long friend)—You will never admit that you followed me to Millersville University of PA, but I know that you did (smile). While I may be in the vanguard, you are such a better version of the North Philly native. Keep up the good work!

Gloria Nyutu Blackman (lifelong friend)—You taught me how to be a true friend. I am forever grateful to you.

Jim Albaugh (best boss ever)—You were my first boss. And, I am so fortunate because you are my best boss. I am blessed to have been influenced by all of your good traits.

Henry Talbert (mentor, advisor, boss)—You gave me my start in the USTA and taught me how to navigate within the organization. I continue to apply daily the lessons that you taught me in the early 1990s.

Special thanks to my wife, Shelia D. Abrams, for the incredible love, support, and creativity that you bring into my life on a daily basis. You are the very best wife and friend a man could have. I love you!

ABOUT THE AUTHOR

D.A. (David Anthony) Abrams is an author, speaker, coach, and advisor who currently serves as the Chief Diversity & Inclusion Officer for the United States Tennis Association (USTA) in Orlando, Florida.

Abrams has been involved in tennis since being introduced to the sport via the National Junior Tennis & Learning program (NJTL) of Philadelphia. As a junior player, he excelled, earning national rankings in the United States Tennis Association, and the American Tennis Association. Good grades along with his hard work on the tennis court earned him a tennis scholarship to attend Millersville University of Pennsylvania. After graduation, he put his accounting degree to good use at Control Data Corporation based in Minneapolis, MN.

Missing tennis, Abrams returned to Philadelphia after four years in the Twin Cities to serve as the Recruitment Director and Head Tennis Professional at the Arthur Ashe Youth Tennis Center (AATYC). While at AAYTC, he launched Dave Abrams Tennis Services, a full-service tennis company that offered tennis instruction to adults and juniors, as well as International Tennis Tours. Abrams has been a certified member of the United States Professional Tennis Association, and Professional Tennis Registry since the early 1990s.

In 1993, Abrams moved to White Plains to join the United States Tennis Association (USTA), where he is now Chief Diversity & Inclusion Officer and moved to their new Orlando headquarters in summer 2016. He has also served in the following capacities: Executive Director of two USTA Sections (Eastern, 2006-2012) and Missouri Valley (1997-2000); Director of Community Outreach (2000-2006); and National Coordinator, NJTL & Minority Participation (1993-1996).

As a board member of the Alzheimer's Association-Hudson/Rockland/Westchester, NY Chapter (July 2009 to June 2013), Abrams served in the following roles: Chair, Audit Committee; Member, Compensation Committee;

Member, Nominating Committee; and Member, Development Committee. In addition, he played an active role in the New York Society of Association Executives (NYSAE; 2010-2011) as a member of the Membership and Education Committees and is a Current Member of the National Association of Asian American Professionals (NAAAP). It should be noted that Abrams is a Certified Association Executive (CAE).

Abrams believes in lifelong learning and loves to read. He also loves to write and, in addition to *The Inclusion Solution: The Big Six Formula for Success*, has written *New School Leadership: Making a Difference in the 21st Century*, as well as *Association Management Excellence: Become An Expert by Preparing for the CAE Exam* and *Certified Association Executive Exam: Strategies for Study & Success*. All of his books are available wherever bestselling titles are sold.

Abrams enjoys travelling with his wife (Shelia D. Abrams) and has visited all of the states within the United States with the exception of four. Countries that he has visited outside of the U.S. include: Australia, Morocco, Denmark, Sweden, Norway, England, China, France, Italy, Thailand, Brazil, Costa Rica, Jamaica, Mexico, Canada, Spain, Indonesia, and the Bahamas.

Over the years, Abrams has made many media appearances, including: "America's Black Forum," hosted by James Brown, to discuss the mission of the USTA's Community Outreach department; a Satellite Media Tour (i.e., 15 Markets across the United States) with tennis legend Zina Garrison, to discuss African-Americans in tennis and the National Junior Tennis League; and CNBC's "Rivera Live," as a panelist, to discuss the impact of Venus and Serena Williams on tennis participation among multicultural groups.

Recent print articles include:

- "Exec of the Future: D.A. Abrams—Different Strokes" (http://associationsnow.com/2012/09/exec-of-the-future-different-strokes/); and
- "Serving Up Diversity: The USTA's D.A. Abrams—Diversity Executive" (http://diversity-executive.com/articles/view/serving-up-diversity-the-u-s-tennis-association-s-d-a-abrams).

Please feel free to connect with Abrams:
Twitter—@DAAbrams1
(https://twitter.com/DAAbrams1)
Instagram—DAAbrams1
(www.instagram.com/DAAbrams1)
LinkedIn—D.A. Abrams, CAE
(*www.linkedin.com/pub/d-a-**abrams**-cae/7/a04/459*)
Facebook—David Anthony Abrams
(https://www.facebook.com/david.a.abrams)

REFERENCES & ENDNOTES

[1] Monster. "5 Companies that are Betting Big on Diversity." *The Huffington Post*. 3 May 2016.

[2] Kondolojy, Amanda. "Disney Channel's 'Sofia the First' Crowned #1 Cable TV Telecast Ever in Kids 2-5".*TV by the Numbers*. 4 Dec 2012.

[3] McDermott, Maeve. "How Disney brought Elena of Avalor's Latin Heritage to Life." *USA Today*. 12 Jul 2016.

[4] Valdez, Jeff. "Baby It's You." *Huffington Post*. 31 May 2013.

[5] Visconti, Luke. "Ask the White Guy: Why White Men Must Attend Diversity Training." www.diversityinc.com.

[6] Bush, Vanessa K., "The Cultural Connection." http://diversitywoman.com. 23 January 2011.

[7] Pirkl, James J. "The Demographics of Aging." *Transgenerational.org.*

[8] Wazwaz, Noor. "It's Official: The U.S. is Becoming a Minority-Majority Nation." *U.S. News & World Report*. 6 July 2015.

[9] Dougherty, Conor and Jordan, Miriam. "Minority Births Are New Majority." *Wall Street Journal*. 17 May 2012.

[10] Frey, William H. *Diversity Explosion: How New Racial Demographics are Remaking America*. American Forum series, University of Virginia. 22 April 2015.

[11] Misra, Tanvi. "Where Minority Populations Have Become the Majority." *Citylab.com*. 9 April 2015.

[12] U.S. Census Bureau, 2010.

[13]Reinan, John. "Lack of Diversity will Hurt your Bottom Line." *MinnPost.* 29 April 2013. www.minnpost.com/business.

[14] "Women of Color in the United States." *www.catalyst.org.*4 Feb 2016.

[15] Council on Economic Advisors analysis of Current Population Survey, Annual Social and Economic Supplement.

[16] Carmen DeNavas-Walt and Bernadette D. Proctor. "Income and Poverty in the United States: 2014" (November 2015).

[17] Bureau of Labor Statistics, Current Population Survey, "Table 39: Median Weekly Earnings of Full-Time Wage and Salary Workers by Detailed Occupation and Sex, 2015." Current Population Survey (2016).

[18] Holland, Stephanie. "Marketing to Women Quick Facts." http://she-conomy.com/facts-on-women.

[19] "Marketers: 80% of Pinterest Users are Female...Is Your Brand There?" www.she-conomy.com/4099/marketers-80-percent-of-pinterest-users-are-female-is-your-brand-there.

[20] "The-top 30 stats you need to know when marketing to women." *TheNextWeb.Com.* 24 Jan 2012. http://thenextweb.com/socialmedia/2012/01/24/.

[21] Dishman, Lydia. "Where are all the Female Creative Directors?" *Fast Company.* 26 Feb 2013.

[22] www.diversityinc.com/diversity-facts. Black History Month "Meeting in a Box" Facts and Figures 2016.

[23] The Nielsen Company.

[24] "Money is Power: Giving Credit to Multicultural Financial Habits." *Nielsen.com.* 25 Mar 2015.

[25] Berovici, Jeff and Pomerantz, Dorothy. "The Next Media Jackpot: The Fight for the $1 Trillion Hispanic Market." *Forbes Magazine.* 6 August 2012.

[26] "Meeting in a Box: National Hispanic Heritage Month." *www.BestPractices/DiversityInc.com*. 14 Aug 2015.

[27] www.DiversityInc.com/diversity-facts.

[28] www.AHAA.com.

[29] Anders, George. "Economic Growth's New Driver: It's All About Latino Entrepreneurs." *Forbes/Tech.* 12 Nov 2015.

[30] Berovici and Pomerantz. "The Next Media Jackpot."

[31] Berovici and Pomerantz. "The Next Media Jackpot."

32 Acuña, Rodolfo F. *Anything But Mexican: Chicanos in Contemporary Los Angeles*. Brooklyn: Verso Books, 1July1995.

33 2010 U.S. Census Bureau.

34 Holly, Don. "What the Numbers Tell Us." *Diversity MBA Magazine*. 19 May 2016.

35 Anders, George. "Economic Growth's New Driver: It's All About Latino Entrepreneurs." *Forbes/Tech*. 12 Nov 2015.

36 DiversityInc.com/facts.

37 *WOW Facts*.12th Edition. New York: Diversity Best Practices, 2012.

38 Steinmetz, Katy. "Why Uncle Same wants to know how many LGBT people are in America." *Time Magazine*. 6 June 2016.

39 Burjek, Andie. "The State of Diversity & Inclusion." *Talent Management magazine*. Jan/Feb 2016.

40 "What does LGBTQIA Mean?" TahoeSafeAlliance.org.

41 The Williams Institute.

42 Kiersz, Andy. "Here are some of the demographic and economic characteristics of America's gay couples." *Business Insider*. 27 June 2015.

43 *WOW Facts*.12th Edition. New York: Diversity Best Practices, 2012.

44 Fuller, Brad. "Here's How Some Brands have Subtly Won Over the LGBT Community." *Business Insider*. 23 June 2013.

45 Lowery, Melissa. "RBC Wealth Management." *Affinity Inc Magazine*. Spring 2015.

46 *Wow! Facts*. 12th Edition. New York: Diversity Best Practices, 2012.

47 "The Next America." *Pew Research Center*. 10 Apr 2014. www.pewresearch.org/next-america/.

48 United States Department of Human Services Administration for Community Living. Washington, D.C.

49 United States Social Security Administration.

50 Packaged Facts.

51 Bhattacharya, Ananya and Long, Heather. "America Still Leaves the Disabled Behind." *CNN Money U.S.* 26 Jul 2015.

52 Bhattacharya, Ananya and Long, Heather. "America Still Leaves the Disabled Behind." *CNN Money U.S.* 26 Jul 2015.

53 "The Next America." *Pew Research Center*. 10 Apr 2014. www.pewresearch.org/next-america/.

54 "The Next America." *Pew Research Center*. 10 Apr 2014. www.pewresearch.org/next-america/.

[55] "The Next America." *Pew Research Center.* 10 Apr 2014. www.pewresearch.org/next-america/.

[56] Dishman, Lydia. "Millennials Have a Different Definition of Diversity and Inclusion." *Fast Company.* 18 May 2015.

[57] Dishman, Lydia. "Millennials Have a Different Definition of Diversity and Inclusion." *Fast Company.* 18 May 2015.

[58] "The Next America." *Pew Research Center.* 10 Apr 2014. www.pewresearch.org/next-america/.

[59] "Meet Generation Z." CBS News Interactive. *CBS News.com.* 2016.

[60] "Meet Generation Z." CBS News Interactive. *CBS News.com.* 2016.

[61] "Meet Generation Z." CBS News Interactive. *CBS News.com.* 2016.

[62] "The Next America." *Pew Research Center.* 10 Apr 2014. www.pewresearch.org/next-america/.

[63] "Meet Generation Z." CBS News Interactive. *CBS News.com.* 2016.

[64] Deloitte. "Re-examining the Business Case for Diversity." Australia, September 2011.

[65] "Diversity: It's Good for Business, and Here's Why." *www.diversityjournal.com.* 21 March 2011.

[66] "Selected Examples of Marketing to Multicultural Consumers." *DiversityBestPractices.com.* March 2013.

[67] "Why Does Diversity Matter?" *www.rbc.com.*

[68] Vasquez, Tina. "Andrés Tapia: Elevating a Buzzword." *Hispanic Executive.* 10 Dec 2015.

[69] Austin, Patrick Lucas. "General Mills: Workforce Diversity High on the Corporate Menu." *Black Enterprise.* Dec 2014/Jan 2015.

[70] Miller, F.A. & Katz, J.H. *The Inclusion Breakthrough.* San Francisco: Berrett-Koehler Publishers, 2002.

[71] Deloitte.

[72] Catalyst. "The Bottom Line: Corporate Performance and Women's Representation on Boards (2004-2008)," 2011; and Catalyst. "The Bottom Line: Corporate Performance and Women's Representation on Boards," 2007.

[73] From 2005-2007, McKinsey & Co, 2007.

[74] Herring, C. "Does Diversity Pay? Race, Gender, and the Business Case for Diversity." *American Sociological Review,* Vol. 74, 2009. pp. 208-224.

[75] Deloitte.

[76] Metzler, Christopher J. "Board Diversity: A Win Win Win." *Talent Management Magazine.* Jan/Feb 2016.

77 Vasquez, Tina. "Andrés Tapia: Elevating a Buzzword." *Hispanic Executive.* 10 Dec 2015.

78 Tulshyan, Ruchika. "Pushing the Frontiers of Diversity." *Diversity Woman.* Summer 2015.

79 "Diversity Leadership: John Lewis." *Diversity Inc.* http://www.diversityinc.com/john-lewis/

80 Ernst & Young Global Limited. http://www.ey.com/GL /en/About-us/Our-people-and-culture/Diversity-and-inclusiveness. 2016.Z

81 Associated Press. "Fortune 500 companies cover sex change operations, other procedures for transgender workers." 24 October 2015.

Human Rights Campaign Foundation. *Corporate Equality Index 2016.* www.HRC.org.

82 Associated Press. "Fortune 500 companies cover sex change operations, other procedures for transgender workers." 24 October 2015.

83 The HRC Staff. "Starbucks Stands Up for Equality and Transgender Rights." 9 Jun 2016. *www.HRC.org.*

84 Associated Press. "Fortune 500 companies cover sex change operations, other procedures for transgender workers." 24 October 2015.

85 Burjek, Andie. "The State of Diversity & Inclusion." *Talent Management Magazine.* Jan/Feb 2016.

86 Carter, D. A., Simkins, B. J., and Simpson, W. G. (2003), Corporate Governance, Board Diversity, and Firm Value. Financial Review, 38: 33–53. doi:10.1111/1540-6288.00034

87 "The 2014 DiversityInc Top 50 Company for Diversity." *DiversityInc.*

88 "Master Steps for the Dance of Diversity." *The Huffington Post.* Posted 4 March 2012.

89 Brown, Jennifer. "Employee Resource Groups that Drive Business." *Jennifer Brown Consulting,* 2010.

90 Parrott, Forrest. "AT&T Employees Confirm: The Company's Serious about Diversity & Inclusion." *www.DiversityInc.com.* 4 May 2016.

91 Brown, Jennifer. "5 Ways to Leverage the Power of Employee Resources Groups for Leadership Development." *Jennifer Brown Consulting.* 15 Sept. 2010.

92 Stahl, Ginter K., Ingmar Bjirkman, Elaine Farndale, Shad Morris, Jaap Paauwe, and Philip Stiles. "Six Principels of Effectve Global Talent Management." *MIT Sloan Management Review*. 1 Jan. 2012.

93 "Workplace Diversity Hindered by Failure to Communicate, Study Says." *Huffington Post*. 8 April 2013.

94 Hom-Franzen, Genny. "Zurich American Insurance lauds diversity and inclusion." *Affinity Inc Magazine*. Winter 2015.

95 "Sodexo: No. 2 in the DiversityInc Top 50." *www.DiversityInc.com*. 2015.

96 Bureau of Labor Statistics. "Persons with a Disability: Labor Force Characteristics Summary." 21 Jun 2016.

97 Monster. "Five Companies that are Betting Big on Diversity." *The Huffington Post*. 3 May 2016.

98 Monster. "Five Companies that are Betting Big on Diversity." *The Huffington Post*. 3 May 2016.

99 http://www.imintohire.org/get-the-facts/

100 "Billionaire Carlos Slim and Best Buddies International Founder Anthony K. Shriver Call on Employers to Pledge 'I'M IN TO HIRE' Individuals with Intellectual and Developmental Disabilities." *www.Best Buddies.org*

101 Strom, Stephanie. "Frito-Lay Takes New Tack on Snacks." *New York Times*. 12 July 2012.

102 Weeks, Matt. "Asians, Hispanics driving U.S. economy forward, according to UGA study." *UGA Today*. 24 Sept 2015.

103 "Most Supplier Diversity Programs Simply Fail to Deliver." The Hackett Group. 14 May 2010.

104 Moore, Ralph G. President, RGMA. *www.RGMA.com*.

105 "A Win-Win: Companies Thrive, Communities Get a Boost With Supplier Diversity." *DiversityInc.com*.

106 "Supplier Diversity a Win-Win: Companies Thrive, Communities get a Boost with Supplier Diversity." *www.DiversityInc.com*.

107 Whitfield, Gwendolyn. "Supplier Diversity and Competitive Advantage: New Opportunities in Emerging Domestic Markers; 6 Strategies for Partnering with Key Minority Stakeholders." *Graziadio Business Review*, 2009.

108 "Most Supplier Diversity Programs Simply Fail to Deliver." The Hackett Group. 14 May 2010.

109 "Supplier Diversity a Win-Win: Companies Thrive, Communities get a Boost with Supplier Diversity." *www.DiversityInc.com.*

110 Heinrichs, Christine Willard. "Finance finds strong diversity programs a help in tough times." *DiversityCareers.com.* Dec 2008/Jan 2009.

111 "The DiversityInc Top 13 Companies for Supplier Diversity." *www. DiversityInc.com.* 2016.

112 www.allstate.com/diversity/supply-chain.aspx#.

113 "Supplier Diversity a Win-Win: Companies Thrive, Communities get a Boost with Supplier Diversity." *www.DiversityInc.com.*

114 www.att.com/gen/corporate-citizenship.

115 "Supplier Diversity a Win-Win: Companies Thrive, Communities get a Boost with Supplier Diversity." *www.DiversityInc.com.*

116 www.staples.com/sbd/cre/marketing/staples_soul/diversity.html

117 "Walmart Creates Value Through Supplier Diversity." *Minority Business News USA.* 1 Sept 2015.

118 "Walmart Creates Value Through Supplier Diversity." *Minority Business News USA.* 1 Sept 2015.

119 Lowery, Melissa. "Nationwide's Andrew D. Walker." *Affinity Inc Magazine.* Fall 2014.

120 "Nationwide Named to the FORTUNE 100 Best Companies to Work For List for the Second Consecutive Year." 3 Mar 2016. *www.nationwide.com/about-us.*

121 Frankel, Barbara. "Diversity Management: 2012 DiversityInc Special Awards." http://www.diversityinc.com/diversity-events/2012-diversityincspecialawards.

122 "Targeting the Best Hispanic Consumer: A Generational and Cultural Orientation Study." AHHA, in collaboration with AARP.

123 "A Fast-Growing But Diverse Hispanic Market." *Wall Street Journal.* 30 Apr. 2013.

124 "Sodexo: No 3 in the DiversityInc Top 50." *www.DiversityInc.com.* 2015.

125 Visconti, Luke. "Interview With University Hospitals CEO Tom Zenty: Diversity Leader, Innovator, Community Citizen." *DiversityInc.com.* www.diversityinc.com/leadership/diversity-leader-innovator-community-citizen/.

126 "Forest City's Chief Diversity Officer Builds Community Support." *DiversityInc.com*. www.diversityinc.com/leadership/forest-citys-chief-diversity-officer-builds-community-support/.

127 "PG&E to Welcome the "Year of the Snake" with Chinese-American Communities." *www.PGE.com*. 12 Feb. 2013.

128 "Black McDonald's Operators Association® Honors Diversity Pioneer Patricia Harris." McDonald's New York TriState. 6 Aug 2014.

129 Cohen, Sir Ronald and Sahlman, William. "Social Impact Investing Will Be the New Venture Capital." *Harvard Business Review Blog*. 17 Jan. 2013.

130 Visconti, Luke. "How to Get Budget for your Diversity Program." *www.diversityinc-digital.com/diversityincmedia*. Feb. 2011. P.12.

131 "Global Philanthropy: JPMorganChase." www.jpmorganchase.com/corporate/Corporate-Responsibility/corporate-philanthropy.htm.

132 Diversity Best Practices Staff. "Partnerships with Special Interest Organizations." *www.diversitybestpractices.com*. 1 Dec. 2011.

133 Diversity Best Practices Staff. "Partnerships with Special Interest Organizations." *www.diversitybestpractices.com*. 1 Dec. 2011.

134 Turner, Yvonne Sui. "The Civic 50: Best Practices in Corporate Community Engagement." *The Conference Board,* 2015.

135 Austin, James E. and Seitanidi. "Collaborative Value Creation: A Review of Partnering Between Nonprofits and Businesses: Part 1. Value Creation Spectrum and Collaboration Stages." *Nonprofit and Voluntary Sector Quarterly*. July 2012.

136 Babiak, Kathy. "The Role and Relevance of Corporate Social Responsibility in Sport: A View from the Top." *Journal of Management & Organization*. 2010:16.

137 "The DiversityInc Top 50 Companies for Diversity survey." www.*DiversityInc.com*.

138 Williams, Valerie. "Wells Fargo Announces its Busiest LGBT Pride Season Ever Media." *www.glsen.org*. 7 June 2011.

139 "Comcast: Inclusion Provides the Competitive Advantage." *Black Enterprise Special Report*. Dec 2015/Jan 2015.

140 "American Airlines and UNCF Launch Gift Card to Help Today's Students Become Tomorrow's Leaders." *American Airlines (www.aa.com)*. Joinus.Aa.com/American-airlines-uncf. 10 May 2013.

[141] "Get to Know your Network: Fiscal Year 2011." *The Consortium for Graduate Study in Management.* www.cgsm.org.

[142] "How Philanthropy Benefits your Company." *www.diversityinc.com.* www.diversityinc.com/diversity-recruitment/the-benefits-of-corporate-philanthropy/.

[143] Matamoros, Brenda. "OBOX's Tim and Thom DeWitt are Making a Difference." *Affinity Inc Magazine.* Winter 2015.

[144] Lowery, Melissa. "Athlete Ally: Promotes Inclusiveness On and Off the Field." *Affinity Inc Magazine.* Spring 2015.

[145] www.AthleteAlly.org

[146] Visconti, Luke. "Why White Men Must Attend Diversity Training." *www.diversityinc.com.* 8 March 2011. http://www.diversityinc.com/ask-the-white-guy/why-white-men-must-attend-diversity-training/.

[147] "Ingraining Diversity & Inclusion in Your Company's Culture, Values and Ethics." DiversityBestPractices.com/news-articles.

[148] Burjek, Andie. "The State of Diversity & Inclusion." *Talent Management Magazine.* Jan/Feb 2016.

[149] https://www.microsoft.com/en-us/diversity/business-of-inclusion/default.aspx

[150] Zeigler, Cyd. " ESPN launches employee LGBT ally program with Trey Wingo, Sage Steele and others." *www.OutSports.com.* 28 Jun 2012.

[151] Rykoff, Amanda. "Wendy Lewis Maintains Diversity Pipeline." *EPSNW.* 10 October 2011.

[152] http://admericaaaf.org/wendy-lewis/

[153] Prinster, Rebecca. "What's Good for Baseball Is Good for Business: MLB's Wendy Lewis Talks Supplier Diversity and More." *INSIGHT Into Diversity.*

[154] "NASCAR Drive for Diversity Unveils 2016 Driver Roster." *www.NASCAR.com.* 15 Jan 2016

[155] Lowe, Frederick H. "As African-American Embrace NASCAR, So Does the Africa Channel." *The North Star News* and *NewAmericanMedia.org.* 7 Jul 2012.

[156] Gaille, Brandon. "52 Fantastic Nascar Demographics." http://brandongaille.com. 17 Jan 2015.

157 Hoffman, Sandy, Randall Lane and Posner, David. "Measurement: Proving the ROI of Global Diversity and Inclusion Efforts." www.Cisco.com/web/about.

158 "Dashboards & Scorecards: What Exactly are They? And Which One should I Use?" Blum Shapiro, Boston, MA. www.blumshapiro.com/media/uploads/files/Dashboards%20and%20S corecards.pdf.

159 Garrett, John. *Facilities Management Advisors, LLC.* www.facilitiesmanagementadvisors.com/.

160 "Prudential Financial: No. 8 in the DiversityInc Top 50." *www.DiversityInc.com/prudential-financial*

161 "Diversity Scoring Tool©: Measuring Your Diversity, Diversity Best Practices." www.diversitybestpractices.com.

162 "How ERGs Increase Engagement." *www.Diversityinc.com.* http://www.diversityinc.com/resource-groups-2/how-ergs-increase-engagement.

163 Burjek, Andie. "The State of Diversity & Inclusion." *Talent Management Magazine.* Jan/Feb 2016.

164 "How ERGs Increase Engagement." *www.Diversityinc.com.* http://www.diversityinc.com/resource-groups-2/how-ergs-increase-engagement.

165 Silva, Betsy. "Diversity & Inclusion: A Strategic Imperative. *The Sodexo Story.*" Sodexo. http.//www.gcpartnership.com/Economic Inclusion/ Commission/Diversity-Professionals/Inclusion-Change-Management-Conference-08-17-11.

166 Robinson, Marcus, Charles Pfeffer, and Joan Buccigrossi. "Business Case for Diversity with Inclusion." Rochester, NY: wetWare, Inc., 2003. http://workforcediversitynetwork.com/docs/business_ case_3.pdf.

167 Bolchover, D. "Re-engaging With Engagement." *The Economist: Economist Intelligence Unit.* Retrieved 17 June 2011. http://haygroup.com/EngagementMatters/Re-engaging-with-engagement.pdf.

168 Source: Gallup, n.d.

169 Cataldo, Pat. "Focusing on Employee Engagement: How to Measure It *and* Improve It." *UNC Keenan-Flagler Business School.* Executive Development 2011.

170 "2015 Latino 100." *Lation Magazine.* Spring 2015.

---

[171] Ladimeji, Kazim. " 5 HR KPIs That Can Boost Business Performance by up to 3X." www.bscdesigner.com. 11 Jul 2015.

[172] Lowery, Melissa. "Lockheed Martin's LGBT ERG Breeds Success." *Affinity Inc Magazine.* Spring 2015.

[173] *CocaCola Journey™:* Our Company—Workplace Culture. http://www.coca-colacompany.com/our-company/diversity/workplace-culture.

[174] Garcia, Eric. "2015 Latino 100/Cigna." *Latino Magazine.* Spring 2015.

[175] "Walmart 2015 Diversity & Inclusion." Global Office of Diversity and Inclusion. http://cdn.corporate.walmart.com.

[176] "MasterCard Worldwide: No 6 in DiversityInc Top 50." *DiversityInc.* Jan 2015.

[177] *MasterCard Diversity and Inclusion 2014. www.mastercard.us.*

[178] "The DNA of Diversity." *Talent Management.* 22 Feb 2012.